T0247774

Praise for
Better Culture, Faster

This is breathtakingly brilliant. Just incredible. I devoured it from cover to cover and loved every word. This book is a complete joy. And it will change your life. It is warm, funny, compelling and astoundingly easy to read – you won't want to put it down. It will rid you of all the nonsense you thought you knew about culture and how to change it. And replace it with everything you need to make your culture the performance accelerant it needs to be for your business. A must read for every leader.

Julie Nerney, Transformation Leader and Non-Executive Director

This very funny book will revolutionize your business. If only I had a business.

Jo Brand, Comedian

When it comes to culture change, Andrew is my 'go-to' expert.

Mark Long, Chief Executive Officer, Ignite

Andrew's approach to culture change is a testament to his deep understanding of the subject. He strips away the nonsense often associated with cultural transformation, highlighting the power of honest leadership and dedicated effort. His book is a practical guide for leaders who want to make a real change in their organization.

Seth Kybird, Chief Executive Officer, NTS

Having seen Andrew in action, this book will be gold dust for any leader or practitioner.

Mark Smith, Chairman, Ignite

Andrew provides productive challenge and encourages candour. The net result is an organization unified to deliver the strategy.

Laura Wise, Chief Officer Governance & Risk, NEBOSH

You've written a book? Oooh! It's about business? Why would anyone buy that?

My Mum

Andrew came into our business at a time of life-or-death change – which we were finding difficult to navigate. He gave us the framework, the tools, the skills, the knowledge and the confidence to rapidly deliver the culture changes we needed. Read this book – it will help you do the same.

Laura Peach, Finance Director, Nebosh

BETTER CULTURE, *FASTER*

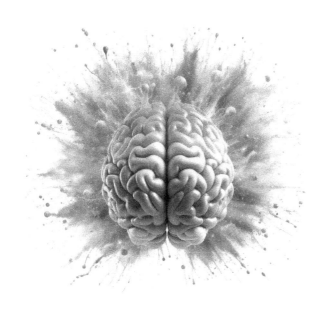

ANDREW SAFFRON

First published in Great Britain by Practical Inspiration Publishing, 2025

ISBN   9781788606868 (hardback)
       9781788606875 (paperback)
       9781788606899 (epub)
       9781788606882 (kindle)

Want to bulk-buy copies of this book for your team and colleagues? We can customize the content and co-brand *Better Culture, Faster* to suit your business's needs.

Please email info@practicalinspiration.com for more details.

Practical Inspiration Publishing

This book is dedicated to all of the people who've truly inspired me. I've never met any of them: this is an unambiguously self-interested, but ultimately certainly futile, attempt to get one of them to phone me.

This book is for Arsène Wenger, PG Wodehouse (not around, but with that brain, probably capable of emailing me from beyond), Michelle Obama, the entire Earth, Wind and Fire band (come on – EVERYONE loves them), Judi Dench, Paul McCartney, Tim Minchin and John Oliver.

Call me…

Contents

Introduction:
Culture – do it, do it now,
do it fast

Everyone's talking about culture at the moment. You hear politicians taking swipes at the culture of another political party, you hear football managers talking about the importance of getting their culture right, you hear about the toxic culture in such and such public service, or some parts of social media, and you hear lots and lots about the importance of an organization's culture. Most of them have a broad view of what this means, but when it comes to doing something about it, most haven't a clue what they're talking about. But at least they're talking about it.

I help organizations to change their cultures and I've been doing it for nearly 30 years. For the first 15 years of that, it was quite a slog to convince my clients that getting their culture right would change everything. Or anything. They thought it was a soft and fluffy subject. They thought it was about putting bean bags in the meeting rooms. They thought it was the same thing as 'staff engagement'. They thought it was what HR does – because they're the ones who know about people.

More recently, organizations have started to realize that their culture will directly impact their ability to achieve their business goals. You might be one of those who still doesn't believe that. Read on.

However, despite the fact that there's greater enlightenment about the behavioural contribution that people make to performance, there's still a lack of understanding about how to change the culture. Which is fine. That's how I make a living. But that's where this book comes in: it will tell you what culture is, how it affects business performance and will give you a step-by-step instruction manual for how to define what changes you need to make to your culture, how to make those changes *and* how to change your culture rapidly.

Rapidly? Really? Yes. I know all the textbooks tell you it takes years to change your culture. I know that most leaders you speak to will proclaim confidently that it will take years. But what about my clients whose performance is plummeting and don't have years to change? What about my clients who have amazing ambitions and want to, or need to, achieve them far, far sooner than far, far later? The answer is that culture can be changed rapidly. It's true, there is a direct correlation between the size of the organization and how long it takes to change the culture. The bigger you are, the longer it will take to reach the fingers and toes of the whole organization. But it does *not* need to take years. Nor should it. I'm going to describe a step-by-step process for rapid culture change. All of the steps need to be followed rigorously. You can't skimp or skip. You wouldn't skip from step two to step ten in your self-assembly furniture instructions.

In this book, I'll pull no punches in telling you what works and what doesn't. I know how to blow a huge amount of your organization's money on all kinds of complete waste-of-time activities. I know how you can spend years trying to change the culture… and fail at it. I know how you can get a reputation for being the person who puts posters of your organization's values round the walls, giving everyone a nice new mug with the brand spanking new values printed on them… and who delivers the square root of absolutely nothing.

I also know how to massively reduce your spend, deliver huge culture shifts in short periods of time and how to get a whacking great slap on the back for doing it.

I've been delivering culture change in private and public sector organizations all over the world for the best part of 30 years. I speak the truth. Which might feel painful. Particularly if you've just done something like blown 25% of your budget on a complicated culture assessment tool that no one understands; or sheepdipped 500 people through a one-day training course, designed and run by trainers who have never actually run any part of an organization; or spent ten months with expensive consultants to define the exact wording and font size for the values that now adorn the walls of your office that everyone ignores… perhaps tutting in exasperated fashion as they pass by.

In this book, I'm going to cut through the dunghills of bullshit about culture. I'm going to help you differentiate between the really good ideas and the cowboy charlatanism. I'm going to eliminate the crap and show you what you need to do.

In other words, you might actually *like* to hear the truth. By telling you the truth, I'm going to save you time, save you money and most importantly of all, I'll show you how to actually change your organization's culture, both significantly and rapidly.

This book doesn't extend to hundreds of pages. Why? Because culture change is *not* hard. Or at least the method is simple. Changing people's individual and collective behaviour *is* hard. But that will happen if you use the right method.

There are also other reasons for keeping this short and sweet. Choose the reason(s) that apply to you:

1. **You've never actually read a management textbook to the end.** Because, let's be honest, a lot of them are pretty dry and dusty. And once you've got the gist, you stick a post-it note into the page that has a quote or a graph that you're definitely going to use in a presentation at some point in the future. Which probably doesn't happen; but the faithful post-it note adheres to its task. In five years, you retrieve the book from the shelf and the post-it note has faded and it's a bit battered at the edges. But it commands you to find the line on that page that you really liked when you read it five years ago. But you can't find that line and wonder why you wasted a good post-it note on it. Poor post-it note.

2. **We live in a TikTok world.** Our attention spans are shrinking faster than your bank balance during eleventh-hour Christmas eve shopping. We have so many things vying for the attention of our overloaded brains: 150 emails a day; meetings… endless bloody meetings; presentations to the Executive Team; team cascade comms; customers; staff; the bloke who sits near you who won't stop chatting/flirting/sniffing/asking your opinion; printer jams; the school calling to say your kid is ill and needs to come home; more emails; more meetings in which you swear you can actually see your soul leaving your body.

   No wonder our health is taking a turn towards the emergency room. And while I'm on the vitally important subject of mental health, why, oh why, oh why are organizations all talking about 'resilience'? 'We must help our people be more resilient.' Er, hang on, instead of getting all het up about your staff's well-being in the face of the mountains of rubbish you tip in their direction every day, how about talking about changing the effing things that cause their health problems in the first place? It's a bit like approaching a man who is slowly sinking into quicksand and asking him if he'd like a nice quinoa and kale salad.

Fix the culture, fix the mountains of rubbish. Fix the culture, fix the time spent in meetings where people neither contribute value nor derive value.

3. **You have a life.** I realize that the number of you reading this, who could reasonably and accurately say that you have a life to call your own, is diminishing. See the second point above.

But for those of you who have fashioned a small corner of your waking hours to be with the people you love, doing the things you love, this book is for you. I'm reminded of my favourite apocryphal quote by Winston Churchill: 'Say what you need to say, shut up, sit down.' A good rule for life, I think. Who cares whether he said it or not. And next time you're having dinner at a team building event and you've been sat next to the person who only stops talking about themselves long enough to ask you to pass the water, feel free to use this quote on them. Both barrels.

This book says what it needs to say. And then shuts up.

PART 1

Why getting your culture right will change everything

Chapter 1

What is culture anyway, and why does it matter?

Let's start by being clear about what culture is. Here's a definition I heard at a client's leadership conference:

> Organizational culture is a system of shared assumptions, values and beliefs, which governs how people behave in organizations. These shared values have a strong influence on the people in the organization and dictate how they dress, act and perform their jobs… To quantify the relationship of individual behaviour with group norms, research in organizational behaviour often frames it as $B_{i} = f(N_{G})$.

I don't know about you, but I don't find that particularly helpful. Probably it's fantastic to help you with a theory essay you might be writing for your MBA, but in the real world, it doesn't help you to start building a project plan.

Here's another definition:

> Organizational culture encompasses values and behaviours that contribute to the unique social and psychological environment of an organization.[1]

---

[1] David Needle, *Business in context: An introduction to business and its environment* (2004).

Come again? I mean, I understand the words, but it doesn't help me to know it when I see it, why it matters nor what to do about it.

I'm going to come back to the word 'values' later in the book. Suffice to say, at this stage, I hate it. The word has been so overused and abused that it's been rendered useless. Textbooks about culture are full of drivel about values and are regurgitated as if they're facts. The true meaning and relevance of values has become buried and blurred, and yet just about every FTSE 100 company will have a set of 'values' hanging around on the walls, like 17-year-olds at a nightclub on a Saturday night.

'OK', I hear you say. '*You* tell us what it is. Dazzle us with your wisdom.'

'OK, I will', I reply calmly (but inwardly, I'm feeling twitches of petulance, ready to fire off a volley of shots over the heads of the crowds of textbook junkies and word-swallowers).

So, in a nutshell, here's what I know about what organization culture is: it's the unwritten rules for how we behave in a particular organization. I realize that sounds incredibly simplistic. And, obviously, the rest of this book significantly expands on that. But while the definition is short, it's vital. The fact that these rules are *unwritten* makes it difficult to readily grasp what they are. And the fact that they're 'rules' tells us that people do abide by them – probably unconsciously. So what? Why does behaviour matter? Because those behaviours dictate how decisions are made, whether continuous performance improvement is even possible, whether unifying dots can be joined across the organization, whether you can retain talent, whether you're able to move at pace and whether you're able to focus on what's important to your customers. All of which tells us we're grappling with something that will have a life of its own unless we're willing and able to get a good double-handed grip on what's going on.

Let's look at a couple of examples of where these 'unwritten rules' have taken the driver's seat in organizations. In a global defence organization I've worked with a lot, they historically had a culture of aggression, abrasiveness, blokeishness and combative internal competition. An investment bank I worked with recently had a culture of gossiping and bad-mouthing behind people's backs. In a global telecoms organization I've worked with, they now have a culture of 'helpfulness', i.e. we really love mucking in to help each other out to get the job done and hit the targets.

No one tells them to behave like this, they just do. And newbies to the organization do it because we all have an ability to chameleon-like blend into our environments (or choose not to, and leave).

But here's my favourite definition of culture (and this is a post-it note bookmark moment):

A monkey's tale

Put five monkeys in a cage. Inside the cage, hang a banana on a string and place a set of stairs under it. Before long, a monkey will go to the stairs and start to climb towards the banana. As soon as he touches the stairs, spray all of the monkeys with cold water.

After a while, another monkey makes an attempt with the same result – all the monkeys are sprayed with cold water. Fairly soon, when another monkey tries to climb the stairs, the other monkeys will try to prevent it.

Now, turn off the cold water. Remove one monkey from the cage and replace it with a new one. The new monkey sees the banana and wants to climb the stairs. To his horror, all of the other monkeys attack him. After another attempt and attack, he knows that if he tries to climb the stairs, he will be assaulted.

Next, remove another of the original five monkeys and replace it with a new one. The newcomer goes to the stairs and is attacked. The previous newcomer takes part in the punishment with enthusiasm.

Again, replace a third original monkey with a new one. The new one makes it to the stairs and is attacked as well. Two of the four monkeys that beat him have no idea why they were not permitted to climb the stairs, or why they are participating in the beating of the newest monkey.

After replacing the fourth and fifth original monkeys, all the monkeys that have been sprayed with cold water have been replaced. Nevertheless, no monkey ever again approaches the stairs. Why not?

Because that's the way it's always been around here.[2]

Good, isn't it? Pop the post-it note in.

Just to be clear, this wasn't an actual experiment. No animals were hurt in the writing of this book. But as I looked into the

---

[2] Gary Hamel and C. K. Prahalad, *Competing for the future* (1996), although I think it's an old fable that they copied.

provenance of this story, I discovered that there are stories out there about this being an actual experiment. But that's total rubbish. It was never an experiment, but some people have taken it as true. And doesn't that sound like some of the nonsense at work where we accept things as 'the way we do things round here', even if we think they're ridiculous?

Not convinced? You're thinking 'that's monkeys – humans don't follow the crowd like that?' Wrong. Derren Brown did an experiment some years ago that demonstrated exactly the same point as the monkey's tale (google 'Derren Brown Compliance Test'). In the video we see a bunch of people turning up to a waiting room for a job interview. Already in the waiting room are three people who are filling in a form. They're actors. And they've been told that when they hear a bell ring, they should stand up. And when you hear the bell ring again, sit down. And repeat every time you hear the bell. One by one, more job applicants are taken into the waiting room. When they see the three actors stand when the bell rings, the new applicants stand too. And when the bell rings again and the actors sit down, the new applicants sit down too. They don't know why. Unconsciously, they think: 'That's just the way things are done round here. Those are the unwritten rules. I'd better conform.'

Here's another example. This one is entirely real and entirely true. I worked at a hospital some years ago that had a rule that if you drove to work there, you parked in the staff car park, walked into the building and went to work. However, if you cycled to work, you were required to put your bike in the bike shed and then sign in at reception to declare that you'd put your bike in the bike shed. One of the doctors I was working with was fascinated by this weirdness and looked into it. She discovered that the reason for this was that during the Second World War, when not many people had cars, if you cycled to work there, you registered this at the front desk, in case cyclists were needed to deliver messages and supplies in the local area. No one challenged this until she did. Seventy years of an absurd process. Accepting that 'that's just the way we do things round here' without questioning.

Hopefully that helps clear up what culture *is*. But I realize that it doesn't answer the question of *why* an organization's culture is important, why it matters, why it's critical to business performance. Read on.

I've just given some examples of the culture I've found in various organizations over the years. But do all those sets of behaviours necessarily mean that the culture is bad? I mean, does the culture I just described of internal combative competition necessarily have a negative impact on performance? Nope. It might be exactly what's needed.

You might have spotted something important there: I talked about impact on performance. I didn't talk about 'good' or 'bad' cultures. Culture must not be referred to as 'good' or 'bad'. *It's about whether your culture helps you or gets in your way.* This point is critical (post-it note on standby):

The only purpose in talking about culture is to decide whether it will enable you to achieve your strategic goals or get in the way of it. Put simply, does your culture enhance your organization's performance or inhibit it?

Here's an example that I think might illustrate the point. I was working with a high-tech, Silicon-Valley-based company recently. They had a pervading culture of perfectionism. Sounds great, doesn't it? But actually, they were going bust. The reason? Because they polished and polished and polished before taking new products to market… by which time their competitors had already got out there, mopped up the market, had a celebratory dinner and drinks in the pub and spent their bonuses on a weekend in Paris.

Does your culture enable everyone to do things faster, better and cheaper? If yes, good. If not, you'd better get cracking.

That's why you've heard the expression 'culture eats strategy for breakfast'. It doesn't matter how good your strategy is. No matter how leading-edge, how professionally managed the programme is and how market-shifting it might be, it won't happen if your culture gets in the way of everyone performing in the way you need them to. Because it's the *people* that have to deliver the strategy. I know that's obvious. But I thought it was worth mentioning because that rather important fact can surprisingly get ignored in the first flush of a love affair with a new strategy, or a recovery plan, or product launch or expansion plan.

OK, one last example in case you're trying to avoid the truth. A leading insurance company I worked with had a brilliant strategy to pretty much smash and grab the market from their competitors in only one year. It was so good that when you read it, the only appropriate response was 'someone fetch a Pulitzer for the author of this'.

But they were struggling because at the same time as adding cool photos to their 'Strategic Road Map' document to be issued to all staff to engage them in the new strategy, their customer satisfaction and therefore Net Promoter Scores were fading faster than the friendship you made with that couple on holiday.

Customers at the insurance company weren't happy because when they phoned the call centres, they couldn't get their issues resolved first time. And that's because they had a completely unempowering culture. If empowerment means 'devolving decision-making authority to the lowest, most appropriate level' (and it does) then decisions here were being made two or three levels above the call centre agents. The call centre agents didn't have the decision-making authority to give customers what they needed. They were seriously irked, so were their bosses who were drowning in operational treacle (and therefore couldn't retain any degree of strategic focus) and so were the customers. The shiny new strategy would be like setting off on a sea voyage when you have holes in your boat.

So once again, does your strategy enable people to perform or does it get in their way?

Chapter 2

How to analyze your organization's culture in eight minutes… and three vital conclusions about culture

Hopefully, so far, it all makes obvious sense. So, let's just spend a moment to tie this directly to your organization and your culture. But before we do that lets look at your possible situation.

Your situation

Let's recognize that the principle I described in the previous chapter of *optimizing your culture in order to improve performance* applies in all situations. The two main reasons that I get called in to help organizations evolve their culture are:

1. **The organization is struggling.** Performance is suffering (anything from stumbling a bit, to falling off a cliff).

2. **The organization is successful.** Performance is good, but it needs to improve. This might be because the competition has got its running shoes on, or market

conditions have changed or strategic targets have grown significantly (as a result of success).

In both situations, every one of the principles and tools described in this book apply. Culture will drive performance. That's it. So, it therefore doesn't matter in which direction performance is trending.

An example of a struggling organization that needed to change its culture: I recently worked with a business that had a cost base about 50% higher than any new entrant would have. Performance had entirely plateaued for a few years and was now starting to move in a downward direction. The Executive Team recognized that they needed to change the way they operated or they wouldn't exist in about five years. They recognized the urgent need for greater empowerment, unified thinking and action across and within the business units and to move at a far greater pace. They applied these 'culture imperatives' and performance is now climbing.

An example of a successful organization that needed to evolve its culture: I recently worked with a $2.4bn business that had aspirations to become a $3.6bn business within five years. Achieving a 50% uplift in top-line performance meant that they had to resolve the 'growing pains' that were starting to beset them. Growth pains are good pains because they are born of success. They knew that they couldn't keep doing things in the way they'd always done them, because a) their scale prevented this; and b) their customers were looking for them to be more adventurous, less risk-averse and more fleet of foot. They applied core principles of smart risk-tasking, fail fast and solid outcome ownership, and they've already beaten their strategic targets.

Analyzing your organization's culture in eight minutes...

Let's now make this entirely specific to your organization.

Do this. Honestly, do it. You can do it in the bath, on the train or over a coffee and a pain au raisin. Just do it. I call it a culture analysis exercise. Because it is. I guarantee in about eight minutes you'll have enough insight to know what needs to be tackled. And after this chapter we'll go on to *how* to tackle it.

1. Take a sheet of paper, draw a line down the middle and label one column 'positive' and the other column 'negative'.

2. Take a few minutes to list words that describe the positive and negative features of your current culture.

   The list doesn't have to be exhaustive. The first words you use will almost certainly be the key points. That's why they've come first to mind.

   By the way, you might have found yourself writing the same word in both the positive and the negative columns. That's common – a culture feature such as 'collaborative' is often written in both columns because in some teams it's very evident but it's not true of all teams. Or it's true in certain situations (e.g. when you're fire-fighting), but not all situations.

   Now look down the negative column and for each negative feature, write next to it words to describe the impact of that negative feature on the performance of the organization. Does it slow you down, cost you money, detract from quality, impact customer service, create duplication of effort, etc.?

Do the same for the positive column. This step should only take another few minutes.

3. Lastly, look at all the words you've written in the negative column (the negative features and their impacts on performance). Looking across them all, now list the few key things you would do to remove the negative features of the culture – and therefore to eliminate their negative impact on performance. The trick here is to not censor your thoughts. Don't censor on the basis of what you've seen done before. Don't censor on the basis of what you think your organization/Chief Executive Officer (CEO) has the appetite for. If you were in charge and you could do absolutely anything, what would you do to get rid of the negative features?

4. You could also spend some time thinking about how to accentuate the positives. But honestly, it's the negative stuff you need to dedicate your mental run-time to. These are the things that are holding your organization back. Like trying to run a hundred metres with a giant rubber band that's tethered to a wall with the other end tied round everyone's waists. You'll make progress (for a while), but it will be hard. Having said that, you must pay attention to ensuring you don't lose the positives (babies and bath water[1]). And having said *that*, I've worked with lots of organizations

---

[1] This refers to an old expression 'don't throw the baby out with the bathwater'. In case you're etymologically minded, the phrase originally comes from a German proverb coined in the 16th century.

who kid themselves that the positives are real. They talk about how 'collaborative' they are, when the reality is that one department doesn't have a clue what the other departments do and/or are perpetually angry with the Finance Department for not being aligned with their needs and/or teams that have to work together to achieve goals that don't have joined-up Key Performance Indicators (KPIs). They might also talk about how wonderfully innovative they are, when actually people are scared of suggesting ideas. For now, this is OK – just brainstorm and list the 'positives'. But later, applying an honest eye over the list becomes critical.

You can draw some critical conclusions from this very quick analysis.

Conclusion number 1: culture is not a 'soft' subject

In case you weren't listening, culture will absolutely prevent you from hitting your targets or it will absolutely help you to hit your targets. It's not a soft and fluffy topic. When I asked you to list the impacts of the negative features on performance, I'll bet you listed some pretty hard-nosed issues like increasing costs, alienating customers, damaging quality, damaging productivity, etc. And you got to that conclusion after about six minutes.

However, I've seen it treated as a soft subject many times. The scenario goes like this: the CEO and Executive Team get the latest employee opinion survey results. And they're not good, for example 71% of staff don't trust the leadership of the organization. So, the CEO says something like 'I know what we should do. We should have one of those culture change programmes. That'll cheer them right up.' And then promptly says to the HR Director, 'all yours.'

There are two fundamental flaws in that version of how to do things:

1. It's not about making staff happy. It's about performance. That's it. It so happens that you do need 'happy' staff so that they're willing to perform, but it has to start with a clear focus on organizational performance.

2. Giving the culture change programme to HR to run is insane. Not because HR are rubbish, but because it's rather silly to ask a support function – who, by definition *support* the business, not *run* the business – to lead a significant shift in the way things get done. And at the same time, you've essentially told the organization that you're not taking this seriously by lobbing it over the wall to HR. Culture is a day-to-day operational issue and it should be in the hands of the people that are running those operations.

Conclusion number 2: culture = behaviour PLUS infrastructure

When you listed the things you'd do to fix the problems, you probably described process and structural issues as well as behavioural things. You may have said that you need to change the organization structure to align what some people do with what other people do. You may have said that you need to change the way people are incentivized. You may have said that you need to change and/or streamline some of the processes that get in the way of people performing optimally. You might have said that you need a more helpful set of KPIs. You might have said you need more useful data.

If you try to tackle behaviour on its own, you'll probably fail because your infrastructure will prevent people from using the behaviours you need. For example, telling people to be more empowering or empowered isn't going to do it. You also need to tackle the processes and policies that prevent people from being empowering/empowered. The insurance company I talked about earlier that was suffering from a lack of empowerment in their call centres spent the GDP of a small nation state on a one-day training course for all staff… to show them how to be more empowered. Within about 3.5 nanoseconds of returning to their desks and putting their headsets on, they bumped into policies, procedures and processes that absolutely prevented them from behaving in that way.

Likewise, if you only tackle the infrastructure, you can end up with a beautiful, shiny new set of processes or a state-of-the-art customer management system that's only as good as the people who are operating them.

Conclusion number 3: Did anyone mention posters?

In your list of things you'd do to fix the culture, you probably didn't list putting posters of the values on the office walls. Or giving everyone a mug with the values printed on them. It's not that those things are rubbish. They might well raise awareness. But if that's all you've got, I suggest you go off on long-term sick leave or run away. Now. Before they catch you.

As I go into new clients' buildings, I glance at the ubiquitous values posters on their walls. And I picture an employee walking past these new decorations who stops at the poster stating 'COLLABORATION – we work together to serve our customers' and thinks to himself 'ohhhhh! That's what I should do! I've been behaving like a total arse for the last three years… but now I know what they want!' And then meditatively strolls away wondering if this explains why he hasn't had a pay rise or promotion in years. And then of course dismisses that as a ridiculous idea – it's not about me, I'm OK. It's others who are the problem.

PART 2

The five steps to a better culture, faster

Chapter 3

Why this methodology works

This is how to change your organization's culture rapidly. It does not need to take years. I've used this methodology many, many, many times. And it works.

There are five steps:

STEP 1:
Define and Decree

the behavioural standards you expect of everyone

STEP 2:
Excite and Educate

everyone about how to embody and embed those standards

STEP 3:
Exert and Enable

performance by aligning your infrastructure

STEP 4:
Assess and Advise

people's performance against those standards

STEP 5:
Reward and Reprimand

positive and negative performance

The next five chapters go through each step in more detail. But before we move on, let me explain why this methodology works. And most importantly, why it will change your organization's culture quickly.

Reason it works number 1

Applying positive and negative consequences is the silver bullet. It's the thing that will give your culture change programme teeth. Asking, encouraging, nudging, even inspiring people to change will not work unless there's a reason they have to. Good things will happen to you if you do perform in the way that we need (career progression, pay raises, etc.). And bad things (no career progression, no pay rises or even getting booted out) will happen to you if you don't use the required behaviours.

You might be thinking that your superbly crafted 'case for change' will do all the encouraging and motivating you need. You're right that this is very important. But it's only half the answer. The case for change argues why you're embarking on your transformation programme. But it doesn't explain how you need people to change and it doesn't then hold them to account for those behavioural standards.

If you do it right, the only people who won't like it are the ones who aren't performing and will therefore be disadvantaged by the system. Good. That's the point. Everyone else will love it. Really love it. Wouldn't it be nice if our people could go home not feeling grumpier than a physical education teacher who never got to play for their country. Going home no longer grumpy because that person in the next department just doesn't do what they said they'd do. Or when they do, it's so poor that you have to stay late, miss dinner with your kids (again) and fix the problems they've caused/re-write the presentation they've produced/re-do their numbers/start from scratch.

When I speak at conferences about culture change, I often start by asking the audience how many of them have ever had a boss who was a bit of, or quite a bit of, a jerk. Let's say there's 300 people in the audience. Just about everyone puts their hand up. Have you just metaphorically raised your hand?

Then I ask how many of them would describe *themselves* as a jerk of a boss. No one raises their hand. (Did you?) Actually, that's not true. There's always one. Don't know why. 'Yeah, I'm an arse. Can't help it.' But this of course allows me to make the following point: if most of you have worked for a jerk of a boss and none of you would describe yourself as a jerk of a boss, the chances are that some of you are wrong. You might be right that you're an exceptional, talented boss, or you might be wrong because you don't understand your impact on others.

Which brings me to *the* biggest point about trying to change people's behaviour:

We tend to think that we're OK and other people are the problem.
And even though I've just said that many of you, in your heads, have probably just said something like 'yeah, that's true Andrew, but in my case… I *am* OK! And it *is* other people who are the problem!'

See? It's a major obstacle to behavioural change, which is why you need to compel people to change by applying positive and negative consequences.

Reason it works number 2

It tackles the behavioural *and* the infrastructural issues that impact performance. As I've mentioned, you can't, for example, ask and train your people to behave in a more empowered way, when the processes, delegated authorities, systems access to sign-offs or your governance structures absolutely prevent them from behaving in that way. You can't ask your people to work in a more collaborative way when the processes squeeze out the need to, or time for, working with others who have valuable insight; and the Key Performance Indicators (KPIs) are not joined up/don't incentivize working together.

Reason it works number 3

The methodology is progressive. It doesn't stand still. The behaviours you need today might not be the behaviours you need next year or the year after. Because markets change, customer expectations change, your people's expectations of the way their organization is led change and technology changes the way you have to get things done. This methodology allows you to re-define the required behaviours and easily change the system you use to measure whether people are using them.

The next five chapters will go through each step in detail, breaking down into why it's important and providing an instruction manual for how to do it.

Chapter 4

Step 1 – Define and Decree

STEP 1:
Define and Decree

the behavioural standards you expect of everyone

STEP 2:
Excite and Educate

everyone about how to embody and embed those standards

STEP 3:
Exert and Enable

performance by aligning your infrastructure

STEP 4:
Assess and Advise

people's performance against those standards

STEP 5:
Reward and Reprimand

positive and negative performance

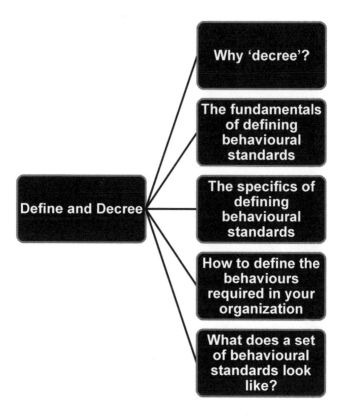

This is about defining the behavioural standards you expect of everyone. And then decreeing that their use is mandatory.

Why 'decree'?

But hold on a minute... 'decree'? Isn't that language a bit strong? Do we really want to *decree* that these are the standards we expect everyone to live by?

Yes.

Think of it this way, would you tolerate someone who came to work at 10am, did the crossword, took a two-hour lunch and then cleared off home at 3.30pm? No, of course not – those aren't the standards you expect everyone to live by. So why would you tolerate behavioural performance that isn't in keeping with the standards you need to drive the business forward? You probably have standards for your kids – don't leave your dirty clothes lying around, contribute to making and/or clearing up from dinner, be polite to your grandparents. And you might insist on those standards. Same thing. These are your family's behavioural performance standards… it's a decree.

I promised you no bullshit, no punches pulled – so decree it is. You might not choose to use that word when you're talking about this. It's not the *word* that matters – it's the intent. Your every action needs to be based on this being mandatory, a decree. Gentle nudging or diffident requesting will only tell people that you're not really serious about this.

When Mikel Arteta took over as the Manager of Arsenal Football Club, he knew he had a culture challenge. I don't know the ins and outs of it, I wasn't there. But he clearly understood this principle. There were some behavioural issues in the team, so he decreed his required standards and when two of those superstars didn't listen, he sold them.

The New Zealand All Blacks rugby team famously have a mantra of 'no dickheads [in the dressing room]'. Meaning, it doesn't matter how technically gifted you are, if you can't behave in a way that contributes to enhancing the performance of the team as a whole, you don't get into the team.

A friend of mine is a theatre director. She operates on the same principle – she chooses not to work with actors who have a reputation for being 'difficult'. Even if they're extraordinary actors.

This chapter now divides into two parts: the fundamentals and the specifics of defining the behavioural standards you need in order to achieve your business goals.

There are some fundamentals in behavioural standards for all organizations. These apply whether your organization is large, small, commercial, public sector, manufacturing, services... every type of organization.

The specifics are about the specific behavioural standards that your specific organization needs at this specific point in time.

The fundamentals of defining behavioural standards

Let's start with first principles. And the grandfather of all this stuff was Jack Welch at General Electric (GE). He came up with a model that describes great performance as being not just about great 'task ability' (your ability to do the job it says you were hired to do in your job description) but also about your behavioural skills (which roughly translates as 'what's it like to work with you?').

It's critical to recognize that by focussing on the ability to do the job you were hired to do, as well as the behaviours (how you go about doing it), you should be seeking to achieve the *multiplier effect*.

Let's build to that conclusion by exploring each of the quadrants of this model in a bit more detail. Understanding the implications of being in any of the four quadrants is essential to significantly and rapidly changing your organization's culture.

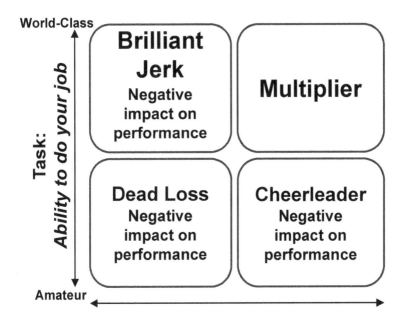

One quick thing before we get into it: the behaviour scale doesn't describe a range from being a horrible person (Blocker) to being a lovely person (Empowerer). It's not about nice and nasty – although it's tempting to read it that way. Imagine you have someone working for you who is under-performing, and you have to have a difficult conversation with them about their performance. The person on the receiving end of that conversation probably isn't thinking you're a 'nice' person. But having that conversation puts you firmly at the high end of the behavioural scale because those are appropriate, empowering behaviours. Avoiding that conversation is inappropriate, blocking behaviour. So, in effect you can be at the low end of the scale because you're too 'nice'.

Bottom-left quadrant: Dead Loss

How would you describe what it's like to work with or for someone in the bottom-left quadrant? I imagine you'd say that it's irritating, frustrating, makes your life harder, etc. And if you were to ask yourself what impact this person has on the performance of the organization, you'd be forced to conclude that, in a word, it's 'negative'. They don't do their job properly and they get in the way of others doing their job properly. And if this is your boss, you and others in the team are probably having to do their job for them.

So, what would you do with them? If you were their boss, how would you fix this? Certainly, you'd start by giving them some straight feedback and a time period in which to develop their task and behavioural skills. You might give them some kind of training. You might give them a coach. And hopefully that will move them into the top-right quadrant.

But what if they don't make enough of a shift? Well, put it this way: imagine your organization was privately owned and that you're the private owner. That means that every Friday afternoon all staff have to come to your desk to get paid. You take out your wallet and give them your money. How long would you be happy doing this for? Your answer to that question was probably something along the lines of 'not bloody long'.

So, why do we tolerate these people having a drag-factor on other people in organizations?

Sometimes the answer to that question is that we end up tolerating them because the organization doesn't have a good enough set of HR practices to enable you to manage them appropriately. You might be thinking that managing someone out of your business takes so long and ties you up in so much HR bureaucracy that it's not worth it. And sometimes the answer is that managers just don't have the bottle to do it.

Neither is acceptable. It can't be. It's not about being nasty to anyone. In fact, it's the opposite – it's about looking after the people who are getting damaged by the negative performer. It is an absolute truth that 'people join a great company and leave a poor manager'. If this person manages other people, they will be negatively impacting at least a half a dozen people's job performance... and lives. If your organization's HR practices are getting in your way, fix them! And don't take 'oh, no, we have to do it this way' as the final answer. It's usually not true. And if you don't have the courage, there's some tools in Chapter 10 that will help you.

Don't forget, it's also about empowering the under-performers by giving them the information, and hopefully incentive, to change.

A client of mine, the CEO of a global manufacturing organization, recently put it this way to all staff: 'If you're performing in the bottom-left quadrant, we'll give you feedback and help you to change. But if you don't, we'll say thank you for your years of service and goodbye.' Spot on.

Bottom-right quadrant: Cheerleaders

What's it like to work with or for these people? You might thoroughly enjoy their company but ultimately, they're not performing. If you work for them, you might think they're great at first (particularly if they've just replaced someone who was horrible) but it won't take long before you realize that because their task skills aren't up to scratch, they can't set direction, can't challenge you, can't answer your questions. You can't learn from them and they can't create an aligned, cohesive, purposeful team. So, if you had to describe the ultimate impact of these people on performance, you'd have to say that at first it might be positive and then it will drift through neutral but end up being negative.

What should we do with these people? Again, I quote the CEO of the major global manufacturing organization. He said about these people: 'We'll give you feedback and help you to change. But if you don't, we'll say thank you for your years of service and goodbye.' The same message, the same principle applies.

Top-left quadrant: Brilliant Jerk

This is the tricky one. Because you could argue that, because of their great technical skills, they're actually adding something to the organization. Yes, they might add something… at first. But I believe – in fact, I *know* – that this is a short-term thing. It doesn't take long for the impact of these people's poor behaviour to start impacting other people's ability to do their job. Here's two examples to prove this:

- A hospital in which some of the surgeons were described as being the 'best in the world' at what they do – but absolute assholes to work with. Which places them firmly in the extreme top-left corner of our model. You might wonder what on earth could be so bad about their behaviour that it's not massively compensated for by their brilliant technical skills. The answer is this: some of the theatre nurses told me that when they were in the operating theatre with these surgeons, they would sometimes see the surgeon doing, or about to do something, that might endanger the life of the patient. But they would be too afraid to say anything because they were too scared that the surgeon would shout, complain and seek retribution.

- In a big public transportation organization, the performance of one of the Directorates was tailing off. It had been the top performing part of the business, but it was falling, and falling fast. When asked to investigate by the CEO, we discovered that the man in charge of this Directorate wasn't what they had assumed. He had achieved incredible financial results, and everyone had assumed he was wonderful. But in fact, he ruled by fear. He didn't physically hurt people. But the emotional scars borne by those who worked for him were deep. The result of this was that about 60% of the people in this Directorate were either about to leave or were just about to join. And the net result of this? Fewer and fewer people knew how to do the job. It was like someone had pulled the plug out of the bathtub of corporate memory. No wonder performance was dropping. One man, costing the company millions and losing their best people.

To what extent would you tolerate Brilliant (or even 'pretty good') Jerks working in your organization? Again, you'd give them some feedback, give them some support and some time to change. But ultimately, I argue vociferously that no organization can tolerate the impact of these people on others' performance. They might be very good at what they do, but a) they get in the way of others doing their job; and b) they'd do a significantly better job if they could forge strong working relationships with others.

Many organizations have been enlightened enough to understand that some of these people are brilliant, but just aren't great with people. They're not jerks. Sometimes it's personality, sometimes it's life experiences and sometimes it's neurodivergence. These enlightened organizations have recognized that they want to retain these brilliant people by building career paths for them that don't require people/team leadership. By the way, my family is full of neurodivergence. Technically, I'm the only neuronormative one. But the weight of numbers in the family suggests that they're the 'normal' ones and I'm the odd one out. An understanding I try to bring to every interaction I have with people – every time I get all judge-y – is I try to see the human being behind the behaviour.

The CEO of the global manufacturing organization once again said about these people: 'We'll give you feedback and help you to change. But if you don't, we'll say thank you for your years of service and goodbye.' Of course, no one believed him. And then over the next six months, he kicked out his Human Resources Director (HRD), his Chief Operating Officer (COO) and two internationally renowned senior leaders. And the culture of the place started to change very, very quickly. After several days of staff going around the building hanging celebratory bunting, skipping, break dancing and singing 'ding dong the witch is dead', people started working with a far greater sense of freedom, camaraderie, a renewed sense of purpose and a willingness to expend discretionary effort. Why? Because the CEO had stated that he wanted only Multipliers working there;

that he'd get rid of non-Multipliers or give them the chance to perform and develop; he followed through on his promise; and, most importantly, he consistently behaved with courage, treated even the poor performers with dignity (by allowing them to leave gracefully) and therefore stood up as a clear exemplar of the kind of behaviours he wanted. We'll cover Multipliers in detail next.

Mikel Arteta at Arsenal, the New Zealand All Blacks and Jack Welch at GE all understand that Brilliant Jerks have no place in a team.

Top-right quadrant: Multipliers

People operating in this quadrant are having a *multiplier effect*:

Multipliers do *their* job brilliantly well, AND they enable everyone they work with to do their job brilliantly well as well.

Not just their teams. Not just their peers. Everyone. The other people in the meeting they're in. The person from another department who needs some information. The junior person who's learning how to do their job. The project team whose project is going to heavily impact their department. Everyone.

There are many characteristics of a Multiplier. But I think the two most fundamental ones (because they drive most other behaviours) are:

1. **Self-awareness**. Understanding the impact of every-thing you say and everything you do on everyone else.

Someone asked me recently: 'Are you saying that I need to think about everything I say before I say it, and everything I do before I do it?' (You have to read that sentence with the tone of incredulity and disgust with which they uttered it.) My answer was... 'yes'.

2. **Humility**. Being willing to say 'I got that wrong' or 'I don't know' or 'sorry' or 'your idea is better than mine' or 'my plan isn't working'. Humility requires a strength of character that many don't possess. You can see how humility and self-awareness are very closely related. You can't be humble without the self-awareness of what you've done well and what you've done less well on any given day. Being willing to show vulnerability by exposing your weaknesses is often thought of as a sign of weakness. Wrong. It's a sign of great strength.

It can be useful to think about what a Multiplier looks like by thinking about what the *opposite* of a Multiplier would say and do. For example, they find the negatives rather than the positives in someone's argument; they don't do what they said they'd do; they do the bare minimum; they don't engage with their teams; they can be arrogant; they can be weak and timid; they don't challenge; they don't support. I'm going to stop there because it's a very long list and probably you're working with people right now that fit some of those descriptions. Which means you get what I mean.

One last thing about the multiplier effect. If you think about it, the point just above and to the right of the centre of the model is the point of *minimum acceptable standard*.

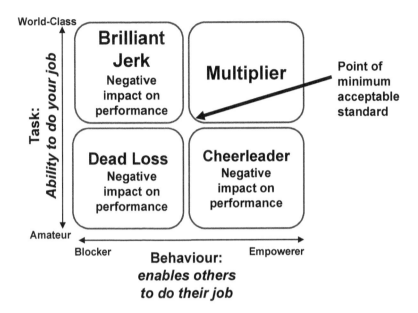

And if that's the point of minimum acceptable standard, then what we're also saying is that, by definition, that's the point of 'mediocrity', which sets out a new performance challenge for your organization: how can we continuously try to raise the performance bar? For instance, if that's the point of minimum acceptable standard, how can we, year-on-year, raise the standard so that the point of minimum acceptable standard continuously rises towards the top-right corner?

The specifics of defining behavioural standards

In Chapter 2, we talked about why you should bother with your organization's culture. In that chapter I suggested that you did an eight-minute exercise to analyze your organization's culture. You might not remember that, so to save you going back, here's a quick summary of that exercise:

1. List the positive and negative features of your organization's culture.

2. For each of the positive and negative features (but especially the negative features) write down words that describe the impact of that negative cultural feature on the performance of the organization (e.g. slows us down, creates duplication, costs money, impact on customer service, etc.).

3. Now take all the negative words (descriptions and impacts) and list the things you'd do to remove them if you had carte blanche. (You can do the same with the positive words, but it's the negative stuff you need to deal with urgently.)

No doubt you'll have written words like bureaucratic, hierarchical, silo-working. You did? How did I know? Because I've run this exercise many hundreds of times in several hundred organizations, and I often hear the same things. The reasons for mentioning that are:

- **Spending money on complex culture assessment tools is not necessary**. Yeah, I know it can give you lovely sacksful of data you can use to a) persuade the Executive Committee to invest in culture change; b) baseline where the culture is now, so you can measure whether it's shifted; and c) build a nice relationship with a big international consultancy firm… in case you want to jump ship. Or need to jump ship if you get this all wrong. But you simply do not need to spend bags of cash and valuable Rome's-burning time on complex and generic culture assessment tools.

- **There's no need to invest in complex tools that analyze your culture to the last behavioural nuance**. Most organizations' cultural issues have similar roots: there are usually cultural issues around how people work together (collaboration) to optimize outputs and outcomes, the quality of their work (for internal and external customers), the ability to continuously improve (call it being 'inventive' if you must) and the style of interaction within the organization (kind, compassionate, helpful, friendly, etc.).

Don't believe me? Think about the values statements of every organization you've worked in. Or google a few. They'll all be some version of those things.

Getting underneath each of those to work out what's good, and what needs fixing, can come later. For now, just know what your culture imperatives are, i.e. which aspects of your culture do you need to address to enable you to achieve your strategic goals? Some of these complex culture analysis tools will drill deep and give ratings for these elements. For example, they'll tell you that 'internal competition' as a function of 'collaboration' is a '6 out of 10'. Is that good? Is that bad? What's the difference between a '6' and a '9'? Or '6' and a '3'? You do not need to know the root causes at this stage. Getting into this level of detail now a) will slow you down massively; and b) removes that opportunity a bit further down the line to get the people working in the business to define the root causes and solutions… and therefore, own it.

When the need to evolve the culture is a result of business growth, these culture analytic tools waste time and aren't specific enough. Imagine five friends who launch a new digital start-up. If it works, it'll grow. A customer services team is needed. A finance team is needed. More people and therefore more managers are needed. Then someone realizes they need a COO and an FD (Finance Director). The sales and marketing force becomes more important and grows accordingly. Then the organization scales into new geographies and even new related markets. More and more IT systems are bought. Sometimes other businesses are bought – and the IT systems don't speak to each other (and nor do the people). When the five friends started the business, they talked directly to each other in the kitchen of the one that has the biggest house/fewest kids running around. But somewhere along the journey, easy communication across the table became communication by long-distance email. More and more people need to be involved. The growing pains start to hurt as the processes just don't work anymore and the IT systems aren't inter-operable. Bureaucracy, hierarchical decision-making, lack of empowerment and silos are born and seem to develop faster than a reality star's ego.

In this last scenario, do expensive, sophisticated tools give you any more valuable data than you'd get from the exercise I just asked you to do? I'd argue that my exercise gives you just about the best data you could possibly hope for because:

- **You can run the exercise for zero cost with as many groups of staff as you like.** This means that staff are engaged in first of all doing some managed moaning (in other words, getting stuff off their chest[1]) and then defining what's needed for themselves. Rather than it being done by external consultants/HR/a project team (probably constituted of people who've never run a culture change programme before)/any other body that doesn't know the business anywhere near as well as the people you're talking to.

- **It's in their language**. Not the spurious, squeeze-to-make-it-fit-us language of a generic survey, including the completely incomprehensible language of some such culture analysis tools. There's one that's been used for years (I won't write the name down here, for fear of expensive litigation) that only makes sense when you hire the tool owners' expensive consultants to come in and explain it to you. And then you pay them to train your people to explain it to other people. Fractured definitions and inaccuracies ensue at a rapid pace.

- **It asks completely open questions**. This is the opposite of a survey which pre-supposes what the issues are. For example, have you ever reached for a customer feedback card in a hotel and found that it's not asking you about the thing you wanted to complain about?

---

[1] Allowing folks to get stuff off their chests in this way is enormously helpful. It shows that you're interested, you're listening and that you care. It also gives them the opportunity to say what they really want to say so that they can then engage with you with a clear mind. And once their engagement is achieved, they will work with you to fix the problems.

How to define the behaviours required in your organization

Here's how to define the required behaviours in your organization. And then read on, because you might be wondering what the output of all of this looks like.

- **Run the culture analysis exercise.** Get groups of your people together to run the exercise I've described above and in Chapter 2. How many of your folks should you do this with? Well, a friend of mine, the CEO of a well-known global brand, says that to hear a true representative view of what's going on in your organization, the number of people you need to speak to is the square root of n, where n is the total size of your workforce. I like that. It feels about right to me. The only caveats are: a) you, of course, need to make sure that you're hearing from a real cross-section of grades and functions from your organization; and b) if the organization is small, try to get everyone involved.

- **You can run this exercise with pretty much any size group.** Smaller than four is difficult because the people might feel exposed and unwilling to be candid. But otherwise, there's no limit to the number of people in the group you can run this with. The biggest group I've done it with is about 300. They sit at round tables. Each table has a sheet of flipchart paper and a pen on it. You lead them through the steps of the exercise. Reviewing their outputs in a rapid way (you can't ask all tables to report back) requires very strong facilitation skills.

Remember that every interaction you have with individuals and groups is a culture change intervention. The way you run these sessions is really important – at all times, you're role modelling the target culture.

- **Face-to-face engagement of staff in defining the required behaviours is fast, cheap, easy and engages them**. And potentially excites them more than a survey would by a factor of about 298. (I made that number up. I don't need to waste my time looking for research studies that prove what we intuitively know is obviously true.) It's just obvious, isn't it? We have far more valuable conversations with people face-to-face than by anonymous survey. Which, by the way, few people will complete because you've asked them for their opinion on lots of things, and lots of times and you did little or nothing about it. So, why would they complete another survey, when they could do something more worthwhile like lie down in a darkened room, contemplating the meaning of life? How often do you come across fast, cheap, easy, engaging and incredibly effective ways of doing things?

- **Focus on performance**. Remember, at all times, it's all about performance. Creating a high-performance culture. Remember that the only point in talking about culture is to consider the ways in which your culture helps you to achieve your strategic goals and the ways in which it hinders you from achieving those goals. If you lose sight of this, even well-meaning statements like 'we want an engaging, involving culture' don't help. If you seek to create a high-performance culture you will almost certainly need an engaging, involving culture. You've got to start with knowing what you're trying to bake before you start buying the ingredients. Otherwise, it's back to front. If someone says, 'we need a more involving or collaborative culture', ask 'why?' What will greater collaboration do for us? What will it add to our performance?

- **Cheeky addendum to defining behavioural standards: I didn't mention defining your values.** I said I'd come back to this but didn't say when. But there you go. Live with it. We have to be able to live with ambiguity (and other corporate bullshit phrases).

  You might have noticed that nowhere in the discussion above about the fundamentals and specifics of defining your behaviours did I mention defining your values. Most organizations define their values as the statement of the culture they want. So why haven't I?

  The reason is… I hate them. The term has become so overused that it's rendered it unutterably useless. The real meaning, of course, is 'the things that we really value round here.' But if you go into most organizations, they'll have values statements that, broadly speaking, say, 'we value quality, partnership, collaboration and honesty'. And probably something about valuing 'creativity' thrown in. By the way, that creativity thing always makes me frown a bit. I always wonder 'if creativity is the answer, what's the question?' If you know, great. If you don't, you're probably just tobogganing down Mount Buzzword again. Sorry if that insulted you, but this stuff only works if we're willing to face the truth.

The values posters, mouse mats, mugs and screensavers might raise awareness about your intent but lack any degree of specificity about what you expect from people – the required behavioural standards.

Yeah, I know, I know – your values statements have behavioural statements underneath them – probably with gradations of behaviours that vary by level of seniority in the organization. Often this means that everyone has to remember about 46 different things. It's unnecessary complexity. Plus, this is made even more complex when the organization has an existing 'leadership competency framework', which might be doing a really good job of describing the leadership skills needed in this organization (but probably it isn't – most people don't look at them). This additional complexity comes when either a) you now have 46 behavioural standards as well as 64 leadership competencies; and b) someone tries to get around this by merging the two… and hey presto, you've now submerged the culture change imperatives under a huge pile of stuff that you have to work your way through to make sense of. But you don't. Obviously.

So, all of this begs the question, what should a set of behavioural standards look like?

What does a set of behavioural standards look like?

If you want to really, clearly signal change, I'd recommend defining a set of 'culture imperatives'. See how simple that was? The words describe exactly what they are – imperatives about our culture.

Here's the steps to get from today to a robust set of required behaviours.

1. **Define the culture imperatives**. Use the culture analysis exercise, described earlier, to distil out the three to five elements of the culture that will make the biggest difference to you achieving your strategic goals.

    Here's an example following about 50 culture analysis workshops I ran recently for a client:

Culture imperative	Reason it was chosen as a culture imperative
Freedom	A lack of empowerment (devolving decision-making authority to the lowest, most appropriate level in the organization) is slowing us down and detracting from quality. For instance, the people best-placed to make the decisions, because they have the most information, are required to escalate into bottlenecks for decisions to be made by people who know less than the people who escalated.
Helpfulness	We do not work effectively across organization boundaries. Teams celebrate when they achieve goals, even when it is at the expense of other teams achieving theirs. We do not share performance measures, resources or ideas in service of common goals.
Mastery	We operate on a principle of jack of all trades and master of some. We need to be world-class market leaders in our areas of subject matter expertise. 'Good enough' must be replaced with 'how good could we be?' We do not put enough effort into the long-range development of our people and nor do we provide resources and processes that are specifically designed to enable them to perform.

Three culture imperatives. Easy to remember – and the second column is a useful reminder of why this needs to change. Note that the second column calls a spade a spade. It doesn't dress anything up for fear of looking weak. If we don't talk about it, we can't fix it, *and*, best of all, it uses all the words that your people have told you during the culture analysis exercise.

By the way, the word 'helpfulness' can seem, at first glance, somewhat insipid. But my experience suggests that it's one of the most important distinguishing features of a high-performance culture and organization.

2. **Add a strapline for each culture imperative.** The strapline must:
   a)   capture the essence of the change; and
   b)   signal that change is coming.

Back to the example:

Culture imperative	Strapline
Freedom	We have the autonomy to define and execute what's best for us and our customers.
Helpfulness	We collaborate purposefully and serve consistently.
Mastery	We are confident, curious and innovate continuously.

3. **Add guiding behaviours for leaders.** Some culture change initiatives are:
   a)   process-led (change the processes and behaviours have to follow);

b)   systems-led (change the systems and it will require different behaviours to be used); *but*

c)   most are leadership-led (the culture changes when the leaders change their behaviours in leading individuals, teams and the organization).

It's therefore vital that we give leaders very clear guidance about what those required behaviours are. Maximum of four per culture imperative. Any more than that and you risk over-complicating things. If you can't boil it down to four or fewer behaviours, you probably haven't understood what the problem is.

Back to the example:

Culture imperative	Strapline	Required leadership behaviours *As a leader,*
Freedom	We have the autonomy to define and execute what's best for us and our customers	• I will empower others to make decisions. • I will set clear parameters for individuals' decision-making. • I will challenge and resolve unnecessary complexity. • I will encourage and enable the team to look for performance-enhancing opportunities.
Helpfulness	We collaborate purposefully and serve consistently	• I will encourage positive challenge and feedback to continuously improve results. • I will ensure that I am available to those who need my support. • I will build a supportive environment where people can be themselves. • I will place customers and service at the heart of decisions.

Mastery	We are confident, curious and innovate continuously	• I will take measured risks to progress the organization in the marketplace. • I will encourage everyone to fearlessly generate ideas and ensure everyone is comfortable with 'fast fails'. • I will celebrate successes and new ideas that didn't work out. • I will ensure that continuous learning is part of the process and custom of the team.

Remember, though, that the leadership behaviours are there to guide leaders. They should not be expected to memorize them. The engaged leader is the one that refers to this list to make sure he or she is doing what's required to optimize business performance.

Also, please note that these behaviours relate to this specific organization. They focus on the specific issues that this organization was facing. They are not therefore a panacea. The behaviours you define should not be generic leadership skills – they MUST focus on the specific culture challenges you have.

4. **Add guiding behaviours for everyone**. You can now add another column that describes the behaviours you need for everyone (not just leaders). For leaders, this column is in addition to the leadership column. It's not just for non-leaders.

Culture imperative	Strapline	Required leadership behaviours *As a leader,*	Behaviours required for everyone *As a team member,*
Freedom	We have the autonomy to define and execute what's best for us and our customers	• I will empower others to make decisions. • I will set clear parameters for individuals' decision-making. • I will challenge and resolve unnecessary complexity. • I will encourage and enable the team to look for performance-enhancing opportunities.	• I will take responsibility for my area of expertise. • I will keep things simple without compromising results. • I will hold myself to account for delivery. • I will strive to maximize my contribution to the business and to the people we serve.
Helpfulness	We collaborate purposefully and serve consistently	• I will encourage positive challenge and feedback to improve results. • I will ensure that I am available to those who need my support. • I will build a supportive environment where people can be themselves.	• I will act with openness, humility and respect. • I will exercise empathy in the face of disagreement. • I will challenge myself and others to get a better result.

		• I will place customers and service at the heart of decisions.	• I will actively seek views from those who might see things from a different perspective.
Mastery	We are confident, curious and innovate continuously	• I will take measured risks to progress the organization in the marketplace. • I will encourage everyone to fearlessly generate ideas and ensure everyone is comfortable with 'fast fails'. • I will celebrate successes and new ideas that didn't work out. • I will ensure that continuous learning is part of the process and custom of the team.	• I will actively seek to adopt successes from elsewhere before seeking to invent. • I will speak up when I spot risks and opportunities outside of my control. • I will experiment to improve, without fear of failure. • I will look for what can be learned from successes and attempts that haven't worked.

And that's it. You now have a set of required behaviours that you can use as the basis for the Excite and Educate work in the next chapter. Everything now refers back to this. This is the North Star for the culture change work. It should also serve as the North Star for any other programmes and initiatives that are going on in your organization. For example, if you're going through an organization design process, the design principles should directly relate to the culture imperatives. Using the example above, the new organization design should inherently enable freedom, helpfulness and mastery.

Do not now complicate your beautifully simple picture of the target culture by complicating it with layers and grades – for instance, this behaviour looks like this if you're grade X and it looks like this if you're grade Y. This seems to have become common practice, so people now think that it's essential. It isn't. It gets in the way. I recently worked with an organization that had ten key leadership behaviours. Each of the ten had four sub-levels. And each sub-level had seven sub-sub-levels. You don't need me to comment on the viability and usability of that model. Don't do it. The more difficult you make it for readers to interpret the statement of required behaviours, the less likely it is that they'll read them and use them. In fact, disinterest increases exponentially as the picture becomes more compli-cated. Which means that at some point before reaching the end, the reader's head will go 'tilt' and they'll close the document.

Chapter 5

Step 2 – Excite and Educate

STEP 1:
Define and Decree

the behavioural standards you expect of everyone

STEP 2:
Excite and Educate

everyone about how to embody and embed those standards

STEP 3:
Exert and Enable

performance by aligning your infrastructure

STEP 4:
Assess and Advise

people's performance against those standards

STEP 5:
Reward and Reprimand

positive and negative performance

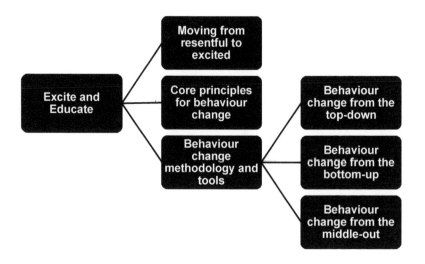

Moving from resentful to excited

This is about a) exciting people about the culture changes; and b) educating them in how to behave differently. Think about how much harder it will be to do b) if you haven't done a).

In this chapter, I'll describe the core principles for changing behaviour, and then I'll describe a tried, proven and trusted methodology for helping people to change their behaviour.

But first, let me justify such a non-corporate word as 'excite'. Can you really excite people about a corporate transformation programme? Or more accurately, can you really excite people about *yet another* corporate transformation programme?

The answer is that while you definitely won't excite everyone, nonetheless it should be your aim. Imagine it the other way around: you want to implement a new enterprise-wide system or streamline all your core processes or evolve your culture so that you can become number one in your market and your starting premise is 'we need to engage everyone in what we're doing.'

Engagement is good. But that suggests either a willingness to join the party or at least not to be negative. How much better would it be if people were actually excited about the changes, if they were genuinely looking forward to the changes, if they went home and told their partners about this exciting new stuff that's coming? And the answer to 'how much better would that be?' is 'loads'. Because this kind of 'better' will lead to faster implementation, faster take up and faster benefits realized.

You might be thinking that I'm in la-la land. You might be picturing the people around you and questioning whether they could ever get excited about change. And your assessment of them might be right. However, working on the basis of there's no point trying to generate excitement means you're aiming to achieve something a bit more than indifference. Instead, try thinking about who these people are, what they want, what they need and give it to them. Getting from folded-arms-over-my-dead-body to grinning excitement won't happen overnight. But to get benefits realized faster means giving it a really good go. Very, very commonly, I've found that the biggest block to people being willing to even listen is that they've told you previously about issues that need fixing. And you haven't. They will not even engage unless you fix these known issues. A giant retail chain I worked with a few years ago was told by the people working in their stores that life would be so much better for them if – wait for it – they had toilets in the stores for staff. No one had done anything about it. When senior leaders tried (and failed) to change the culture, they were surprised by the levels of 'negativity' amongst their front-line store workers. Really? This was a surprise? You treat people with contempt by not listening to what's causing them problems and you expect them to get all excited about another corporate initiative? And then you describe them as being negative. Nice.

So here's a really simple methodology to get from resentful to excited:

1. Fix known issues (gets you from resentful to 'OK, I'm listening').

2. Explain why they should care – how this will benefit them and their customers (gets you from 'OK, I'm listening' to 'OK, but you'd better have a good plan').

3. Demonstrate that having fixed the big stuff, you're now really interested in what else would really add value for them and their customers… and then act on it (gets you from 'you'd better have a good plan' to 'wow – they're actually interested in what I have to say').

4. Act on their ideas, reward them for it and tell everyone about it. Word will spread like wildfire that you'll get noticed by *les grands fromages* if you put your hand up and do something.

There's a caveat here. And it's a good one, because it will keep you and the Executive Team on their toes: if you raise expectations and then don't meet them, you might end up worse off than you were before.

I'm really not in la-la land. You might be picturing excitement as being people wiggling with joy. That's not what I'm talking about. My definition of excitement is getting people to be really, really interested in what you're doing and being willing to throw themselves at it. If you've cleared the known issues, genuinely listened and acted on their ideas, you stand a far greater chance of the organization moving in unison.

Core principles for behaviour change

How do you encourage, help and enable people to change their behaviour? In a way, this is the million-dollar question. We're all different. We all behave in ways that are informed by everything we've learned in our lives. From how our parents behaved and how they made us feel about ourselves in the world, to the social circles we move in, to the people we've worked with and for over the years.

So, shifting the way someone thinks and behaves is pretty damn challenging. But it absolutely can be done. Everyone has the choice to change. And we should help them to make those changes with dignity. What I mean by that is people have been rewarded, promoted and slapped on the back over a number of years for behaving in a particular way. Being told to just do things differently in a judgemental way isn't treating people respectfully or with dignity.

Helping people to change who then refuse to change is a different matter. I'll come to that.

When helping people to change the way they behave, we must be mindful at all times of five fundamental principles.

Principle 1: We're all having an impact all of the time

What we say, how we say it and the way we look when we're saying it (or staying silent) will generate a stack of data that other people will rapidly infuse meaning into. For example, I was told recently after a meeting with my team that I looked bored. I absolutely wasn't – I was genuinely thinking hard about what they were saying, which meant I was (uncharacteristically) quiet. They interpreted this as meaning that I'd switched off because I didn't like what they were saying. What made them think I was bored? They told me it was because I was slouched in my seat. Why was I slouched in my seat? Because there were no clients around, so I was relaxed, and my back was aching. That's not what they saw though. I now make a point of sitting up straight in our team meetings and make sure that my face registers interest (which doesn't always mean agreement) at all times. Yeah, that can be hard when I'm tired or pre-occupied but, boo hoo, it's not that hard. My behaviour – verbal and non-verbal – has an impact on my team so I have a responsibility to add to their performance, and indeed their lives, and not do anything to detract from it.

So why is this a fundamental principle for behavioural change? Because we need to ensure that everyone – especially managers – understand that they will have about 107 opportunities a day to positively or negatively affect other people's performance. Yep, I've made that number up again. But it's that order of magnitude. Don't believe me? Tomorrow, count every single interaction you have with someone at work. That includes your colleagues, the reception staff and the people that work in the staff café.

Principle 2: When we talk about behavioural change, most people tend to think that 'I'm OK, it's other people who are the problem'

This is the biggest obstacle we face when we're trying to change people's behaviour and our culture.

I've mentioned this before but I'm reminding you of it here because it's a challenge that has to inform your thinking throughout the culture change process. It's also a reminder that putting posters of the behaviours on the walls (on its own) is not going to change the culture.

There's a truism at play here: those that need help the most tend to think they need it the least; and those that need it least, tend to think they need it most (because they have a more highly tuned sense of self-awareness).

Principle 3: People have to see the value of changing

Some will just get it. Others will never get it. Some will get it but will (probably with very good reason) say that they've heard it all before and will believe it when they see it. And most will generally see the value but will think it's about other people and not themselves… at this point.

High-quality communications are needed here – particularly if you genuinely want to get people excited about the changes. Here's how *not* to do it:

- Put out a broadcast email from the CEO (that everyone knows they didn't write themself) that gets sped read… but not even that, if they have to start scrolling through the verbose wordage.

- Ask all managers to cascade a PowerPoint document in their weekly comms. Don't need to say much more about that do I? We all know the problems with this. It's even worse in this case, because the culprits of poor behaviour are the most likely to disseminate this important communication badly.

- Invest in an expensive glossy document (written by committee, probably) that sets out the whole plan. This doesn't work because it's one-way communication and it suggests that all plans are already cast in marble and can't be influenced. And spending money on this kind of thing generally raises hackles.

Here's how you *should* communicate:

➤ **Talk to people.** Yeah, really, actually talk to people. Live. Face-to-face. Not much of that around anymore is there? Too many people think that telling everyone on Instagram that they're having a ham sandwich for lunch is communication. But there is no substitute for face-to-face conversation. Which, of course, we all know, but we're all so flat-out busy that we choose a more expedient option. Email, probably. But it's a false economy. You cannot get commitment from an email. Ask a sales person – they'll tell you that if you really want to close a deal, you need to speak to the customer face-to-face. In fact, you could do a lot worse than to consider generating commitment to your culture change programme as a sales activity. You're selling your plan, and you need them to buy it.

➤ **Talk to people.** I know I've said that once already, but it's such an important point, I thought it was worth mentioning twice. I know, I know – how on earth do you get round 10,000 staff in 63 different offices? The answer is that you get the whole senior leadership population to do it with you. I'll give you some more thoughts about this in the chapter about leading culture change (Chapter 9).

➢ **Don't aim for consensus**. Like I said, some people just won't get it. Or won't want to get it. And that's OK. You can't do this by full consensus. If you get it right, you'll influence people as you go along. And, even better, they'll see people around them changing and they'll either absorb what they need to do osmotically, or they'll be picked up in the new performance management system (see Chapter 8). It's vital, though, that you get your most important stakeholders on side. Probably these are your most senior people, but there are other important opinion formers everywhere, including trade unions, the person in Accounts Payable who everyone listens to and front-line people. If they're not with you, they'll potentially poison the well that hundreds of their people drink from.

➢ **Don't assume that everyone in the organization has the same level of excitement about the changes that the project team has**. I've seen this time and time again. The project team sees the future, sees the opportunities, fully understands the plan to get there and maybe has a great Transformation Director who is brilliant at encouraging them to think about the art of the possible and perhaps they even manage to keep their head in the right place when faced with a negative stakeholder. Pretty much no one else in the organization, at programme inception at least, sees or feels any of this. I've experienced project teams

feeling crushed by the indifference or even antago-
nism they feel from the organization. People outside
of project teams can easily start to feel 'done to'. And
to some extent, embarrassed by the project team
because they're thinking about things that they
haven't thought about themselves. Which means
that project teams can become very insular because
they can start to feel different to those others 'who
don't get it'. And the net result of that is some form
of abrasion. And the result of that friction is that it
slows down progress as an unconscious and often
unspoken battle of wills ensues.

Principle 4: You must increase people's self-awareness of the impact of their behaviour on others

We'll talk later about having a 360° (360) tool that helps individuals to understand their performance against the required
behaviours, and we'll talk about having a new performance
management system that provides people with data to help
raise their self-awareness of their impact on others.

But to maximize the impact of those two tools, people also
need a manager who is willing to have completely straight-
talking, honest, high challenge, high support conversations with
them on a high frequency basis. They need to have a behavioural
repertoire that enables them to have straight conversations with
Brilliant Jerks *and* Cheerleaders *and* Dead Losses (see Chapter 4).
My experience, and I imagine yours, tells us that there's a
general paucity of skill in having straight-talking conversations.
Punches are pulled on a very frequent basis. And we also see

those who hold nothing back and deliver it in a 'I call a spade a spade, I speak my mind' unformed, behaviourally dysfunctional way. That version of honesty is just 'littering' – dropping your litter wherever you want.

I'll talk about how to do this, how to do it well and how do it as your default behaviour in Chapter 10, titled 'Caring candour... drives continuous culture evolution.'

Self-awareness and trying to be the best person we can possibly be is, of course, a life's work. One that can be endlessly rewarding and also very challenging. Admitting our own frailties can be very painful. Particularly for us males, who've been trained from the point that we emerged into the midwife's arms to be strong and reveal no weakness. The irony of that (and it took me many years to realize it) is that not admitting weakness is in fact a weakness. We should strive continuously to better ourselves, particularly if we're managers, because we can make a huge difference – good or bad – to the lives of people that work for us.

Therapists and coaches call these 'AFGOs' – another effing growth opportunity. Once you open yourself up to spotting them, they come at you faster than a child on Haribo. But then you learn pretty quickly how to respond to them. And that's when the good stuff happens.

Principle 5: You must give people the guidance they need to change their behaviour

At the risk of stating the obvious, you have to provide people with the support and guidance to change. There are no magic wands. This isn't easy. But there is some fairy dust you can sprinkle to make this work really well and really quickly. So, let's walk through the dos and don'ts of the main tools available to you to help people to change their behaviour.

Behaviour change methodology and tools

I've seen a lot of culture change programmes fail because they operate on a principle of start at the top and hope that everything trickles its way down to the bottom of the organization. This does not work. Ever. Ever. Ever. That's because the messages get increasingly diluted as they trickle down *and*, at about middle-manager level, you'll hit a massive iceberg of an obstacle. Middle managers are likely to block your messaging. Not because they're being bloody-minded (although, of course, some are) but because they don't know why this is happening; they don't fully understand the expectation of them and probably have heard it all before and know that if they just keep their heads down, it'll all go away.

Here's how to get it right. This is the methodology for behaviour change that works. It's harder than a trickle-down cascade, it involves a great deal more effort, but it's also far more interesting, and most of all, it will generate rapid results that will compound over time as more and more people generate the multiplier effect on a daily basis.

The methodology for behaviour change you should be using is:

1. Drive from the top-down
   and

2. Drive from the bottom-up
    and

3. Drive from the middle-out

I'll go through each of these three elements and describe what to do and why each is essential.

Behavioural change from the top-down

Why?

If your senior people aren't actively demonstrating commitment to the culture change efforts, if they're not role modelling the behaviours that are required, if they're not removing infrastructural obstacles to the required behaviours being used and if they're not holding people to account for using the required behaviours, you might as well sit in your armchair, cross your fingers and hope for the best. In a nutshell, if you don't work with the senior people, the rest is a total waste of time.

Who?

In this case, 'senior people' means the Executive Team. If you're a global organization, this is the Global Executive Team. Assuming that the Executive Team includes the leaders of each of your major geographies or operating companies, this might also include, albeit separately, working with each of them and *their* Direct Reports.

How?

There are two key interventions when working with your senior people: team coaching and individual coaching.

1. **Team Coaching**. This type of coaching is about working with that senior team to a) work on their performance as a team; and b) focus on specific actions they will take – collectively and individually – to drive culture change through the organization. I'm not going to go into detail about how to do this here (it's a separate book), but here's some top tips:

    a. These must be very high challenge, very high support sessions in service of helping them to optimize their performance as a team and to drive culture change across the organization.

    This is about challenging and supporting the team about:

    i. How they work together to collectively steward the organization (i.e. taking cabinet responsibility versus attending Executive Team meetings to represent their slice of the organization)
    ii. Holding each other to account
    iii. Giving each other feedback
    iv. How they make decisions
    v. How they represent those decisions when back in the business
    vi. Taking an enterprise-wide view of the business
    vii. The efficiency of their meetings

viii. The quality of the data and papers that come to the Executive Team

ix. The focus must be on optimizing their performance as a team and driving culture change across the organization.

I'm sure you've seen this model before, but just in case, this is what I mean by high challenge, high support and why it matters:

Challenge/support model

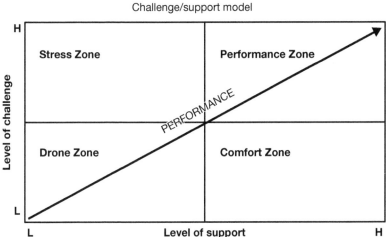

Going softly, softly will not get you where you need to be. Team coaching must start with the coach providing high challenge with high support but needs to get – pretty quickly – to the team being high challenge/high support with each other. Some think that high challenge just isn't 'nice'. But I'm calling bullshit on that. Sitting there internally rolling your eyes about something someone else is doing or saying and thinking judgemental things about them without voicing your concerns is *not* 'nice'.

b.   Ensure that the team engages in 'positive conflict'.

Positive conflict means disagreeing with positive intent, i.e. telling someone you disagree with their idea, approach or opinion with the sole intent to make things better. It's not about challenging/ disagreeing because you want to big yourself up or knock the other person down. I like using the word 'conflict' just because it's a bit provocative... many people think that conflict is a fight. But if you think about it, a conflict is actually just a difference of opinion.

Think of it as it's shown in this diagram of the spectrum of conflict:

The zone of positive conflict is where we innovate, challenge to improve and get better results

Artificial Harmony	Area of positive conflict	Obstructive Aggression
Polite and unhelpful		*Rude and unhelpful*

At one end of the spectrum of conflict is 'Obstructive Aggression', which is perhaps loud, shouty and finger-pointy. You might hear 'that's stupid' or 'you don't know what you're talking about' or 'you're completely missing the point'. It's rude... and unhelpful.

At the end other end is 'Artificial Harmony'. You might hear 'I'm not angry' or 'if that's what you want to do' or 'no, that's absolutely fine' (which is very similar to 'no, that's absolutely fine, darling' that you may hear at home – same shit, different building). It might sound polite, but it's also unhelpful.

In the middle is the zone of positive conflict – this is where the magic happens. It's where we work together to build on each other's ideas (or take them off the table) to get to a better result than we would have done if we were working on our own. There are two component parts to that: a) giving your views with genuine positive intent; and b) receiving that feedback non-defensively. Both elements will need focus when the team is being coached.

In this zone, you might hear 'that's interesting... and what if we changed that bit to this' or 'I don't think that will work because of X... here's my alternative' or 'this is where I've got to, what are your suggestions to improve this?'

c. Use external team coaching experts.

Internal people will not be able to provide the level of challenge required for obvious reasons... which middle-ranking manager is going to face down the CEO and tell them that they're behaving badly? They might be highly qualified and experienced team coaches, but they cannot coach upwards. Apart from anything else, it's not fair on them to put them in a position of potential jeopardy.

2. **Individual coaching**. The team coaching interventions should be supported by one-to-one coaching. This provides the space for the Executive Team members to focus confidentially on their own performance. Again, there a gazillion books about this, so here are just a few top tips for one-to-one coaching:

    a. Make sure you understand what coaching is, what it isn't and what it can do for you.

        In summary, coaching is about all of us continuously developing ourselves. And coaching isn't about something you only do for under-performers.

        It used to be the case that if you were given a coach at work, it meant you were a remedial case – and you didn't tell anyone about it. You probably met them off-site, at the nearest motorway service station in case you were spotted.

        Thankfully, we live in more enlightened times now and we understand that having someone to really challenge you to improve your performance (including if you're already really good) is an extremely valuable thing. If you think about it, even Usain Bolt had a coach. He was the best in the world at what he did. In fact, he's the best that has ever lived at what did. And yet he still had a coach. Why? Because the two men standing next to him at the winner's ceremony want the really shiny medal that he's flaunting. And also, I'll just bet that the psyche of that man says 'how good could I be?' He's driven by a need to continuously improve and seek the edges of his full potential.

b. Choose your one-to-one coaches carefully and wisely.

There are loads of people out there who call themselves coaches. Some are superb and will genuinely change your life. Some are less skilled – they don't have the ability to quickly analyze issues and help the individual to identify where and how to improve. I like to bring in coaches who have a psychotherapy background because they're absolutely brilliant at working out exactly and quickly what's going on for an individual and challenging them hard to improve. Working with an expert coach like this is like being punched in the face while having your mum hold your hand and telling you 'it will be OK.' Try it, you'll like it.

By the way, top tip for life: get a coach. Everyone should have one. They'll help you grow, give you a safe space to download, won't let you just whinge without action and will open doors in your brain that you didn't even know were there.

c. Goal focus.

The coaches should be briefed about the purpose and goals of the culture change programme, so that this becomes the focus. All coachees should speak to their boss and peers to get their view of what they need to focus on. To ensure full alignment, the coaches should meet regularly throughout the coaching period. Obviously, no confidences will be betrayed, but any common themes about the team should be identified and fed into the team coaching process. Plus, the coaches can work together to generate improved collective performance in that team.

d. Consider who else might benefit from one-to-one coaching.

You should go as far into the senior leadership population as your budget will allow. Certainly, the ones who have a weak 360 report should have a coach. But just as importantly, the star performers should get one. I'm a big fan of the notion that you should work with people to really build on their strengths rather than try to fix every weakness. We're all different and we can't all be perfect. In fact, the truth is that we can't all be great at everything. I know what I'm good at and I know where my risk areas are. I've got those risk areas to a point where they're no longer threats but definitely won't ever be strengths. So – simple solution – I ask people in my team who are good at those things to help me out with them. Give Andy a massive spreadsheet and he'll spot the patterns and errors. Give Sharon a huge amount of written workshop outputs and she'll synthesize it into a beautifully presented thematic analysis. I work on my weaknesses only to the point where they no longer represent a threat because I'll never be great at them. And then focus on trying to get my strengths to an elite level.

Behavioural change from the bottom-up

Why?

If you get this right, the people who know most about what's getting in the way of them performing optimally will not only tell you what those problems are, they'll also fix them. Engaging people 'on the shop floor' early on will deliver instant benefits and build a bow-wave of engagement.

Who?

If your organization is around 1,000 people big, you could run this exercise for every team in the business. The 'how' bit below describes a simple workshop you can run with teams.

If your organization is much bigger, you might also consider running this exercise for all teams, but you should think about prioritization. High priority teams are a) those that are struggling (for whatever reason, including poor historical leadership or a significant process or technology change that means they need to operate very differently); b) those that are high performing and, with additional support, could become true exemplars for the rest of the business and from whom other teams can copy and paste; and c) those that will deliver the greatest impact on the performance of the organization by optimizing their performance, for example, a critical customer-facing team or a team that can generate significant efficiencies (speed and cost reductions).

Who should run them? The workshops can be run by internal people as long as they genuinely have the right skills… they do not have to be HR. In fact, preferably they won't be run by HR. If senior-ish people from the operations end of the business (including senior leaders and high potentials) run them, not only will you be demonstrating commitment symbolically, but also they will now have skin in the game to ensure that the performance improvement ideas generated in the workshops are followed through.

How?

It's a really simple workshop. I often call them 'process irritant workshops' because it's usually inefficient processes and processes that are not properly joined up across teams that therefore get in the way.

- **Step 1**. Stick two sheets of flipchart paper (landscape) next to each other on the wall. Draw a line from one end to the other. At one end of the line write 'a bit irritating' and at the other end write 'very, very, very irritating'. Using this language tells the team: 'We get it. Stuff is getting in your way.'

  Ask the team to write on sticky notes (one per sticky) something about how they operate that's irritating/getting in the way.

- **Step 2**. Start working through the stickies from the very, very, very irritating end. For each, get the group to:
  a) agree a problem statement
  b) list the root causes
  c) agree actions to address each root cause
  d) allocate owners of each action.

- **Step 3**. When the stickies represent issues that can only be resolved if another team is in the room (i.e. you need to do some proper plumbing to make the work flow better across those teams), take those away and log them. Then organize for representatives of each of those teams to get in a room together and go through the same process (problem statement, root causes, actions).

- **Step 4**. Agree the 'owner' of those stickies that you haven't worked on during the workshop. That person is now responsible for finding the best way and timing to deal with the rest of those issues.

These workshops should last about half a day. They don't take up much operational time and will fix stuff immediately.

Here's a couple of examples.

- I worked with an organization that switched its operation from being fundamentally analogue to digital. Very few of the ways they used to do things worked any more. Invoices were being sent from seven different places in the organization; processes that were simply no longer required were still being done; manual quality checks were still being done even though the new technology was actually doing this for them. In three weeks, all issues were identified. In eight weeks, all were resolved (some actually, within 24 hours). Almost all of the issues were a revelation to the Executive Team. And that's the point. These are the kinds of thing that you'd only be aware of if you're actually doing the job. No job losses were incurred. They moved a number of people into more customer-facing roles (which they loved) and customer satisfaction ratings went through the roof.

- A rail freight company was under-performing. Costs too high. Profits too low. Sales too difficult. They have two major functions: Operations (Ops) (getting trains from A to B) and Engineering (making sure the trains were fit to run). Historically, Ops and Engineering didn't talk to each other. If you'd been there, about ten seconds into the first session, you'd have heard Ops people saying to the Engineering people, 'I had no idea that when we did X it had impact Y on you.' And vice versa. After only 12 workshops, around £10m of savings had been identified, and best of all, they recognized that they were focussing on the wrong goals: Ops thought their goal was to put drivers in trains, Engineering thought their goal was to get maintenance done. Actually, their real and collective goal was to get the right stuff, to the right place, at the right time for customers. This realization completely transformed the way they worked together. The workshops cost them about £9k using external expert facilitators. Cost savings of £10m (which was only the start) means an ROI of about 99%. I mean, why wouldn't you?

Behavioural change from the middle-out

Why?

Middle managers are the ones that either make your culture change efforts work or block them. If they don't know what's expected of them and aren't given the tools to help them, nothing happens. The Executive Team will rely on the middle managers to facilitate change. Similarly, if you've done the bottom-up bit (see above), all of those fabulous ideas, actions and outputs will go absolutely nowhere if the bosses of those teams are metaphorically or literally saying 'do nothing, this will all go away... just like the previous 23 change initiatives.'

I like to think of the three queues here. My feeling is that people tend to fall into one of these categories:

The Three Queues

Those that complain

Those that advise

Those that do

The challenge is, of course, to move as many people as possible from a spectator role (complaining or advising) to a doing role. Last year, we hosted Christmas dinner for 26 people (I know). I reflected to my daughter afterwards that people seemed to fall into one of three categories: those that say 'oh, you must have worked so hard' and then leave their glass, plate and crumbs all over the place; those that say 'would you like some help?' – usually just as you've finished loading the dishwasher for the fourth time; and those that just help because it's completely freaking obvious that some help would be nice. Complaining or advising spectatorship has no place at work, especially during any kind of transformation programme.

Who?

It, of course, depends on the size of the organization, but a rule of thumb is that these middle-out interventions should include the Executive Team's Direct Reports (minus 1s) and their Direct Reports (minus 2s). And go deeper if you need to. A manufacturing business I worked with recently decided to go down to Executive Team minus 4s because this was where the rubber truly hit the road.

How?

This is essentially about building and delivering a bespoke leadership development and action programme that's designed specifically around the culture and specific behaviours you need.

Here's some tips:

1. **Build specific learning interventions for your specific organization**. Design the learning modules around each of the specific behaviours you need people to have. Don't go anywhere near off-the-shelf training/development packages. These are highly unlikely to be focussed on the specific behaviours you need.

2. **Make the learning interventions modular**. If there are four culture imperatives, run a one-day module for each of these imperatives. I call these 'deep-dive' sessions, so-called because they get under the hood of what's really going on and end with real actions to make changes. In order to generate maximum impact on

culture, and therefore performance, deep-dive sessions will include:

a. Why we need to focus on these priority behaviours
b. Existing team/organization strengths against each priority behaviour
c. Team/organization weaknesses against each priority behaviour
d. Root causes of weaknesses
e. Individual behaviours (and therefore behavioural *changes*) needed
f. Practising use of behaviours
g. Collective team behaviours (and therefore behavioural *changes*) needed
h. Infrastructural changes (especially processes) needed to enable people in your function to perform
i. Actions (behavioural and infrastructural) to embed the culture in your part of the organization.

An example of a modular programme: leaders attended in mixed groups (i.e. not their whole teams) for operational reasons. For this reason, we added 'whole leadership team' sessions after they'd attended the deep-dive modules to give them around two hours together to collate and synthesize all the actions and ideas they'd each taken from the modules and turn them into a coherent, culture-embedding action plan for that team. In this programme, the modules:

• Were for senior leaders
• Were one-day workshops – each module designed around one of their four culture principles

- Executives attended too. They organized them-selves so that one of them was always at each module delivery
- Each module ran multiple times in different locations (they are a global organization). Leaders chose dates that suited them for each module.

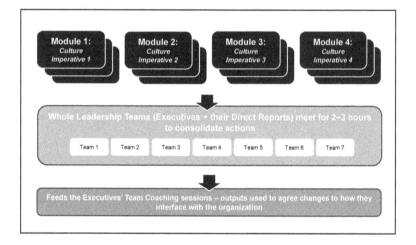

3. **Use absolutely expert trainers**. Don't use generic trainers. And I mean generic in every sense: bland, uninspiring trainers who have no passion for the subject; and generic leadership training-y-type people who do training-y-type things. They're not an expert in culture change and resort to googling culture models from the 1980s. They haven't ever led an organization and can't deliver the development interventions from that perspective. And that will miss about 80% of the value that you should be getting from the development programme. Points (a) to (i) above should demonstrate that the people running these sessions need to have

expert skills as trainers (providing leading-edge input to prompt thinking), as facilitators (being able to tear up the agenda and go with the needs of the group and provide process and structure in a heartbeat to help with this) and as coaches (being able to reflect back to the group the behaviours and the impact of those behaviours in the group).

4. **Go fast**. It's essential (read that word again – *essential*) that you build up a bow-wave of commitment to give the programme momentum. Sending people in groups of about ten to your bespoke development modules, over about a year, is not going to give you the momentum you need because you won't build a critical mass of enough people using the new behaviours that other people then start to absorb. Or the opposite, they get to their allocated development slot, nine months in, and are highly cynical because nothing seems to have changed over the previous nine months.

    I like to run learning events with large groups of people – anything between around 60 and about 180 participants. I know it sounds counter-intuitive, but I really believe that people learn more in larger groups. If you get it right, you can get such an amazing buzz going in the room. One of the best side-effects of this is that the nay-sayers soon start to realize they're in a minority, and the positivists realize they're not alone and that, together, things can change.

5. **Get creative**. Inducing people into a PowerPoint coma isn't really the way to inspire people to change the way

they behave. Nor are syndicate exercises where you send people away into break-out rooms to work on something they have no interest in. And then come back to the main room to present their output to a room of people who had no interest in their own task let alone another group's.

Find interesting ways to get to the heart of the subject. I recently ran a workshop about creating a true service culture. I wanted to talk about putting yourself in your customers' shoes. So I found someone who has to put themselves in their customers' shoes in order to do their job – a close-up magician. What they see is irrelevant. They know how the tricks are done. For them it's all about seeing everything through the eyes of their customers. They were brilliant and the group they presented to are still talking about what they learned. With another client, the big focus was on working together more effectively. So I asked a great friend of mine, who coaches Olympic and Paralympic athletes, to run a session on optimal team working, using the relay race as an analogy for all the component parts. The crowd loved it. He gave them all a relay race baton and asked them to write their biggest commitment on it with a permanent marker. If you visit their buildings now, you'll still see the batons proudly displayed on people's desks.

6. **Make attendance mandatory**. I realize the apparent irony here: that if you're trying to build a culture that's likely to require high levels of engagement and

commitment, telling people what to do right from the start doesn't seem to sit quite right. But the truism I mentioned earlier – the people who think they need this stuff the least, tend to need it the most, and those that think they need it the most, tend to need it least – operates with bells on here. You've got to get people there so you can work with them. One of my favourite methods of doing this without using the word 'mandatory' is an invitation letter from the CEO saying something like 'I strongly encourage you to attend… if you can't attend, please drop me an email explaining why.'

7. **Make it fun**. How come we can remember the gig we went to in 2006 but can't remember what happened in the meeting this morning? Obviously, the answer is that we remember more and learn more when we're fully engaged. And we get engaged when we're enjoying ourselves. I don't mean wearing clown shoes and a red nose or breaking into renditions of Andrew Lloyd Webber show tunes. I mean doing things during the workshop that are utterly compelling. Delivered by trainers who are utterly compelling. A while ago, I attended a training session being delivered by an internal trainer. He laid out toys and silly hats on the tables and told everyone that any time they feel like having some fun, play with the toys. No. No. Just no. Fundamentally, no.

     An utterly compelling trainer:

a. Can tell great real stories to exemplify points. These stories are based on their real experience

b. Understands the context that the group is working in

c. Works only on an adult-to-adult basis. The trainer that operates with a parent–child approach will be met with, at best, indifference, and at worst, animosity

d. Encourages challenge

e. Creates learning activities that require people to move around and genuinely create light bulb moments in the debrief… while having fun.

8. **Get them to do something afterwards**. I like to ask them to come back to the next module with three things that their team are doing differently, now that they're starting to form a high-performance culture in their local area. These might range from getting better quality coffee in the machine to improving the process for project review. It doesn't matter how small the action looks, it's all about them engaging with others to do things differently.

Later, you can up the ante, by getting them to really focus on specific parts of the organization where performance could be enhanced, i.e. getting them to operate in a way that means everyone (*everyone*) understands that it's their job to find faster, better, cheaper ways of doing things.

All of this can look expensive. But I guarantee you a strong and rapid ROI if you follow these rules. Doing it on a shoe-string very rarely works. If people don't see your investment of time and money, they'll think that you don't really mean it. And they'll probably be right.

9. **Make coaching available after 360s** (more information in Chapter 7 about 360s). If you run a 360 (against your culture imperatives and the leadership behaviours that sit behind them) be very mindful that some people will have a difficult emotional reaction (especially if it's their first proper 360 report). They might hear feedback that they've never heard before and conflicts with their own sense of how they're perceived by others. It's essential that you extend a safety net underneath these people in the form of an expert coach who can help them work through first their emotional response and then the detail of the report.

10. **Action learning sets.** Do these things:

    a. Make sure you understand what action learning sets are and the value you can get from them. The key thing you need to know is that action learning sets encourage people to talk about long-term perfor-mance, not just short-term tactical issues. Changes to performance emerge very, very, very quickly as a result of action learning sets.

        Action learning sets are groups of people (who don't necessarily work together every day) that meet on a regular basis to discuss issues and ideas. At each meeting, the members of the action learning set have the chance to discuss a challenge they're facing. The group helps to delve deeper into the issue/opportunity and to find ways forward through strong challenge and high support. Learning set members are encouraged to report back on their progress at the next meeting. If no progress has been made, the group gets into it to find out why and help move things forward. The sets have structure and discipline, but not so much that it squashes free thinking.

The benefits of this are huge. You're basically encouraging everyone to constructively challenge each other so that they can learn and improve. And it encourages people to reflect on their performance outside of the action learning sets too. I was in a black cab in London a little while ago. It was late at night and the driver told me that he was going to go home after he'd dropped me off. I asked him if he's able to go straight to sleep when he gets in or whether he needs to chill a bit first. His answer blew me away. He told me that when he gets home, he makes a cup of tea, and then sits in the armchair and mentally runs through his last six fares. When I asked him why, he told me that he did this to make sure he'd done the best possible job, taking the best possible routes. Wouldn't you like your organization to be full of people like him?

b. Build them into your culture change plan. In other words, ask delegates on the learning modules to form action learning sets after each module. And to report back at the next module about what they've got out of them and what they've done as a result.

c. Use professional facilitators… but only at first. It's a bit daft not to get these off to the best possible start by using a professional action learning set facilitator for the first, say three, meetings. The pros will help the set members to understand the structure, process and value. And I'll bet you ten bucks that after a while, when the pro-facilitators have left, the sets will continue to meet. It happens more often than not because they get so much from them.

Chapter 6

Step 3 – Exert and Enable

STEP 1: **Define and Decree** *the behavioural standards you expect of everyone*

STEP 2: **Excite and Educate** *everyone about how to embody and embed those standards*

STEP 3: **Exert and Enable** *performance by aligning your infrastructure*

STEP 4: **Assess and Advise** *people's performance against those standards*

STEP 5: **Reward and Reprimand** *positive and negative performance*

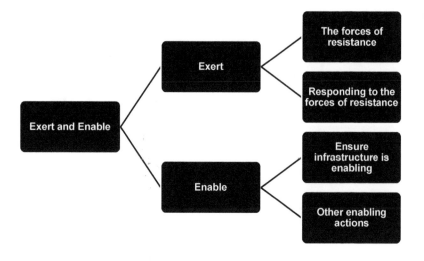

Exert

This is about exerting positive power and influence against the forces of resistance.

The forces of resistance

- **Eye-rolls**. The people who roll their eyes at the words 'culture change programme'. This group of people includes, but isn't limited to, those that have lived through multiple culture change programmes (probably those that extended not much further than putting new values posters on the walls) and delivered little; those that have been banging on about stuff that's getting in their way for years (matrix structures that don't work, non-inter-operable systems or stupid processes that no one has done anything about it), so 'why are you doing this stupid programme instead of dealing with that?'; it's just another tick-box exercise (perhaps because some regulatory body requires it). I completely understand their position. I would probably feel like that.

- **Antibodies**. Organizations are capable of creating antibodies to fight against this new, unwanted incursion. The antibodies are usually generated by those that feel they have something to lose and is therefore driven by fear. The internal Operational Effectiveness team, the Change Management Team, the Transformation Team and HR often feel undermined by a culture change programme. They feel that they should be doing the culture change programme; they feel anxious that they should know how to do it but know they can't (and, by the way, why should they know? It requires a robust methodology and specific set of skills); or they feel threatened because they believe that they do know how to do it and how come they're not trusted with this and money is being spent on external consultants? I've often reflected that if I were working in one of these teams, I'd feel anxious about a culture change team coming in. I can empathize enormously with the antibody generators. It's my job to make them feel heard and comfortable.

- **Brick walls**. The people that aren't interested and don't care. They come off as stubborn jerks, but honestly, they're not. If they're resisting, it's for a reason. It's our job to find out why and exert our influence to win them over. The saying goes that 'no one likes change.' I don't agree. I believe that no one likes change that is done to them, is forced on to them and is tone deaf when it comes to listening to them. It's easy to dismiss these people as irritants. But what if we thought of these people as human beings with all the same worries, threat mechanisms and needs for safety and protection that we have? I consider myself to have a duty of care for these people.

Responding to the forces of resistance

I often hear people talking about the need to 'remove resistance'. I think this is fundamentally wrong. This approach is predicated on 'I'm right, you're wrong.' You might be right… but what if you're not? My approach is to 'embrace resistance' rather than 'remove resistance'. 'Embrace' because they might be right and I might be wrong; they might have knowledge that I don't; they might see risks that I don't; they might have better ideas, and ultimately, adjusting my plan on the basis of what they have to say might lead to a better outcome. And best of all, anyone who makes the transition from resistor to advocate can have a hugely positive influence over others.

There are lots of models and training courses available about how to exert positive power and influence. I won't replicate these here. Suffice it to say that it is essential to respond to the forces of resistance. They can seriously slow you down and, at worst, they can stop you in your tracks.

I find it helpful to think about the source of the resistance. My experience suggests that people resist for one or more of three reasons:

1. Level 1 resistance: I don't know (what you're doing or why)

2. Level 2 resistance: I don't agree (with the way you're going about things)
3. Level 3 resistance: I don't believe (that this is the right thing to do).

How do we respond to each of these three types of resistance?

1. Level 1: I don't know – is easy to deal with. Tell them! Communicate before, during and after.
2. Level 2: I don't agree – is a pleasure to deal with. Listening with Dumbo-sized ears so that they feel heard, and you feel better informed, is a genuinely satisfying experience.
3. Level 3: I don't believe – is the trickiest. Some years ago, I was sent by a client to their HQ building in Germany to meet with their 15 European country managers. The objective was to agree a high-level plan for shutting down 13 of their country manufacturing operations. The session started like this:

Me: 'We're here to discuss the transition plan.'

Them: 'What transition plan?'

Me: 'Er, to shut down 13 country operations and centralize out of the remaining two.'

Them: 'F*@k, sh**' and add another couple of dozen expletives.

They weren't happy because no one at Board level had told them about it. The Board's rationale for not telling them was that this was price sensitive and couldn't risk the information being released into the public domain.

So obviously I hit level 1 resistance – they didn't have a clue about what was happening.

Over the next few months, they allowed us to talk to them about the transition plan and we kept hitting level 2 resistance – they didn't agree with our approach. And they were right. The planners had assumed homogeneity across the 13 sites to be shut down. They were far from homogenous, and the one-size-fits-all plan had to be withdrawn. It's worth mentioning that all through this process, they were understandably very grumpy. Eventually, the plan was executed and completed. Twenty-four months late – because no one had thought about the likely resistance and how it might impede progress. This cost them millions. Over coffee, towards the end, some of the country managers admitted that they didn't believe that shutting down the 13 operations was the right thing to do – level 3 resistance. Yes, they agreed that it was right for the business, but it wasn't right for the communities they operated from and employed people from. They believed a balance between business priority and doing the right thing for the people they were responsible for could have been found.

If someone had trusted them with this price sensitive information right from the start, had included them in the planning, had listened to their alternative thoughts and ideas from the start, a world of pain and cost could have been avoided.

Enable

Ensure infrastructure in enabling

You'll remember that earlier we concluded that culture = behaviour PLUS infrastructure. You can't just tackle culture by trying to change behaviour. You have to change the infrastructure that either enables or hinders people from performing in the way that you want. You can't ask people to act quickly if the organization's decision-making processes don't allow them to do this. You can't ask people to do their best for customers if the systems and procedures don't allow them to do it. You can't ask people to continuously find faster, better, cheaper ways of doing things when there's no mechanism for them to progress their ideas.

Well, you can. But you'd be better off sticking £1,000 on the 250-1 shot in the Grand National at Aintree. In both cases, you're crossing your fingers and hoping for the best. But at least theoretically there's some chance of succeeding if you head for the bookies.

And now I've got good news and bad news.

The good news is that it should be really easy to change the infrastructure. If you ask your workforce to tell you what gets in their way, they'll be able to tell you in less time than it takes you to get your notepad out. They live with it every day. And if you ask them to tell you about it, they'll be happier than an ice cream van man on a freakishly warm day in winter. See the bottom-up section of the previous chapter for how to do this.

But here's the bad news: the processes, procedures, policies that are getting in everyone's way are quite likely to get in the way of you changing them. A very common example I've seen is that organizations know they need to get things done faster but can't get a decision to change the things that'll make things faster because the committee that makes these decisions isn't going to meet for two months, and you're item 29 on the agenda… and likely to get bumped to the next meeting.

In almost every culture change programme I've run, I've found this to be true:

The biggest impediment to the introduction of the new culture is… the old culture.

So what do you do about it? How the heck are you going to get people who are soaked in old culture behaviours to open their eyes just wide enough for you to break through?

I've got four tricks up my sleeve that I use to make this happen:

1. **Process irritant workshops**. See the bottom-up section of the previous chapter. This is the intercontinental ballistic missile in your armoury. If you run these workshops and make sure the actions agreed get done, you've pretty much cracked the majority of the infrastructural issues.

2. **Bureaucracy Busters**. The process irritant workshops might identify the big stuff. But it's more likely that they'll throw up the stuff that affects teams in their areas. Even if they do raise the big stuff, they won't be able to do anything about it themselves because they affect the whole organization. By 'big stuff' I'm talking about

structural issues that cause lack of cohesion; measures/ Key Performance Indicators (KPIs)/targets that aren't aligned across the organization; governance structures that slow people down or detract from quality; project management methodologies; technology issues that get in the way, for example poor quality data, systems that aren't inter-operable and systems that really should replace manual tasks.

To address the 'big stuff', I like to set up a team of people whose task is to eliminate bureaucracy – the treacle that everyone has to wade through to get things done. It's important that the team members have all of these characteristics: smart, proactive, delivery focussed, brilliant at influencing others (including, and especially, senior people) and able to move at speed. The process is easy: you ask your people to submit to the team (using a standard template) the treacle that they want to be removed. The Bureaucracy Busters triage the submissions into three categories:

a. actually can be fixed locally
b. can be fixed but can't be fixed locally
c. low priority or can't be fixed for some good reason (e.g. it's a regulatory requirement).

Then they crack on and fix the category b's and empower teams to fix category a's and go back to the initiators of the category c's to explain – honestly – why the idea can't be progressed. And then the most important bit: they communicate what they've done so that everyone learns to trust the system. Bingo.

3. **Change Council**. Once the organization has got the idea that they can fix stuff and the Bureaucracy Busters have finished, there'll be ideas emerging that people can't implement without approval. Usually this is because either it will cost a lot or it straddles loads of structural boundaries so they can't make a unilateral decision. This is where the Change Council comes in. Think Dragons' Den/Shark Tank. Ideas are submitted to the Change Council and again they're triaged. Then the person with the idea is asked to present to the Change Council, which tries to give them an on-the-spot go or no-go decision. The Change Council should consist of the CEO and at least two members of their team. Along with about half a dozen others who are able to make informed decisions about the ideas.

Whenever I've set this up, I've been blown away by the brilliant ideas that come through. For example, in a railway company, someone had an idea for replacing 17 tools that were used to repair the track with a single tool. They created a prototype in their garden shed. The Change Council bought them a bigger, better lathe (and a bigger, better garden shed) to build the first working model.

Junior people love this because they get to spend a bit of time with very senior people. News of success in the Change Council wings its way rapidly through the organization (with the help of the Comms Team) and everyone really knows now that the culture is dramatically changing.

4. **Culture Change Acceleration Committee**. This is basically the culture change programme steering committee. But don't call it that if the vocabulary smells a bit like old culture. The Acceleration Committee should actually be the Executive Team. But it's important to separate it out so that it has stature and its own governance that won't get winded by the weight of the other Executive Team agenda items. The role of this group is to remove obstacles for the Culture Change Programme Team (including the Bureaucracy Busters). From your mouth to their ears. In order to do this, they have to challenge the Programme Team to make sure it's delivering, delivering the right stuff and delivering at pace.

Other enabling actions

There are two other things that you must do to ensure that the infrastructure enables the required culture:

1. **Align people management practices with the required culture.** That means recruitment, talent management, training and development and, of course, the performance management system (that we'll talk about in the 'Reward and Reprimand' section – Chapter 8).

   a. Recruitment: you've got to make sure you're recruiting people who have the behaviours you require. Gold in, gold out. Simple as.
   b. Talent management: ensuring that star performers have access to roles and development that feels

significantly different to those who don't perform to the required standards. There's nothing more depressing for a hard grafter, who gets results day after day, to know that they're treated no differently from others.

c. Training and development: designed around the required behaviours and delivered to role model the required behaviours.

2. **Physical environment**. I realize that this might not be within your gift to change. But if you can, then start by constructing as many formal and casual meeting spaces as you can. Pretty much every organization I work with at the moment has a shortage of meeting space. You cannot create a high-performance environment when people literally don't have the space to come together to share and bat around ideas, solve problems, capitalize on opportunities or even just hang out and chat.

I came across a company recently that banned coffee at desks to encourage their people to go and chat to each other in the kitchens. I get the intention. But depriving of them of a constant flow of coffee just seems a bit mean to me. Let's not do that.

And then, at the other end of the spectrum, create spaces for people to work quietly on their own. At the very least it means that they don't have to have every MS Teams call with an audience, and at best, it's an opportunity to think without being disturbed.

Chapter 7

Step 4 – Assess and Advise

STEP 1:
Define and Decree

the behavioural standards you expect of everyone

STEP 2:
Excite and Educate

everyone about how to embody and embed those standards

STEP 3:
Exert and Enable

performance by aligning your infrastructure

STEP 4:
Assess and Advise

people's performance against those standards

STEP 5:
Reward and Reprimand

positive and negative performance

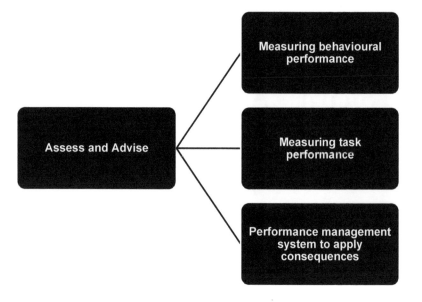

This is about assessing whether individuals are changing their behaviour and giving them feedback. The theory of this is now easy because you know the specific behaviours you need in your specific organization at this specific point in time. The reality is more difficult. I'll talk here about overcoming the first difficulty (aligning your performance management system with the required behaviours). And in the caring candour to drive continuous culture evolution (see Chapter 10), I'll address overcoming the second difficulty – being willing and able to give clear and unequivocal feedback.

In order to align your performance management system with the required behaviours you need:

- An effective tool to measure people's behavioural performance
- An effective tool to measure people's task performance. If you haven't got one already, you need to go and get one (more about how to get one in Chapter 8)

- A performance management system (i.e. the IT bit) and processes that:
  - Collects, collates and analyzes the data
  - Generates automated (prescribed) and manager-discretion consequences for performance (positive and negative)
  - Allows you to enact the positive and negative consequences.

  I'll take each of these three in turn.

Measuring behavioural performance

Obviously, the answer here is to use a 360 questionnaire. In essence, this tool will tell you the boss's, the peers' and the subordinates' views of what it's like to work with this individual. We know that some 360s can be a superb tool for helping someone to move their performance forward. We also know that others can be rubbish.

So here are the absolute golden rules for making sure that the 360 tool works brilliantly:

- **Do not use a generic off-the-shelf tool**. After you've put so much hard graft into defining the behaviours that your organization needs (see previous chapters) why on earth would you then buy an off-the-shelf 360 and then measure people against a different set of behaviours?!

- **Use the behaviours you've defined as being important to the performance of your organization and build your own 360 tool around those**. Ideally, you'd load these into your existing performance management system. But if you don't have the facility/functionality to do that, there are plenty of suppliers who can do this for you quite cheaply. You tell them what behaviours you want to measure – in the form of questions (or some of these suppliers will help you write these questions[1]) – and they'll administer the tool for you, from sending out email invites to click a link and complete the survey to generating individual 360 reports at the end. If you're really desperate for cash, you could even do this manually using paper surveys and a spreadsheet to analyze the data. But don't underestimate the vast undertaking that this will be. I recently saw this done just for the seven-person Executive Team of an organization. The poor souls who did this manually finally emerged blinking painfully as they saw the sun for the first time in about a month.

---

[1] You don't have to be too scientific in your construction of questions – despite the remonstrations of some questionnaire providers who insist that each question must be tested for statistical validity before use. Getting a few people to fill in the questionnaire to test the questions will tell you very quickly whether, e.g. a) they understand them/understand them in the way you intended them; b) you've written some double questions such as 'this person is supportive and challenging' – which one are you asking about? They might be challenging but not supportive. Respondents can't answer both; and c) you've asked about internal *attitudes* that you can't see (rather than specific, observable behaviours), e.g. 'this person believes that communication is important.' You can't possibly know what someone believes. You can only assess the behavioural manifestation of a belief.

- **The reports must be followed up by some high challenge, high support conversations**. I reckon there are three standard responses when people get a 360 report:
  i. absorb, accept, act: 'That sounds about right, I know what to do with that.'
  ii. collapse: 'I had no idea I was perceived so negatively.'
  iii. rationalize away: 'Yeah, I know it looks like everyone hates my guts, but that's only because I was in a bad mood on the day they filled in the questionnaire because I'd forgotten my pass to get into the building and the security guard was mean to me.'

Category (i) response is obviously your lowest priority for support. Category (ii) is your highest priority. We have a duty of care for people who haven't received feedback in this way or of this nature before. Category (iii) is the hardest. But it's really important that we challenge them to fully take the feedback on board.

I was recently asked to coach a male employee in category (iii). He started the session by whacking his 360 report on the table and angrily and arrogantly asking me: 'Have you read that?' I nodded. He said: 'So, basically everyone thinks I'm great.' To which I said: 'Well, I've read the report but why do you have a reputation round here for being an arsehole?' Speaking truth. Meeting fire with fire. He slumped. He muttered: 'Yeah.' And from that we were able to have what I believe turned out to be some life-changing conversations. To be clear – I'm not advocating this as an approach everyone should take! I'd done my research; I knew enough about him to know that this would work. I knew that he was essentially a bully, and that someone needed to stand up to him.

- **Try to avoid people being able to choose who'll complete the 360 questionnaire about them**. Obviously, they might be thinking about the consequences of getting a 'bad' report. So they'll choose their friends to complete the questionnaire. Theoretically, you should know who every individual's boss, subordinates and peers are. That's the theory. But we all know that it can be very messy sometimes. For example, some folks are part of several teams and have several bosses. If your people management system has this information, then great. If not, then you should absolutely be trying to move towards doing this. But in the meantime, you have to do a bit of trusting that people will elect the right assessors; but just to double check, you should ask line managers to give the list a quick once over.

- **Don't have too many questions**. Some of these generic, off-the-shelf 360 questionnaires have 80+ questions. Which is a complete nonsense. Because here's what happens: a manager gets a reminder from HR the night before he's supposed to complete 360 questionnaires on all 12 of his staff. So he sits on his sofa doing them (with one eye on the 10 o'clock news) getting more and more bored, slipping deeper and deeper into a survey coma and starts just ticking down the middle of the rating scale because he's now hallucinating and seeing Big Bird flapping around in front of his eyes. If you're applying consequences for people's performance, you have absolutely no right to do anything except give this your full attention. Read on for more about applying positive and negative consequences.

We should help out by giving them only about 20–25 (maximum) questions to answer. A really tight, focussed set of questions will give you a better result than a large swathe of questions (even if the statisticians tell you that you have to ask each question more than once in different ways to test the validity of the answer).

Measuring task performance

This is about measuring how well someone is doing the job you hired them to do – from HR business partner to operations manager, to finance person, to customer services rep, to factory team leader.

However, I'm going to bust a big myth now. Brace yourself because this is *not* what you've been led to believe for your whole career.

The received wisdom is that the Executive Team members should be set objectives that directly link to the organization's goals. Sure. Makes sense so far. The thinking then goes on to suggest that the Executive Team's objectives should cascade down to their Direct Reports so that they're doing things that are directly in line with the organization's goals. So far so good.

But. The received wisdom goes on to say that this cascade of objectives should flow right down to the bottom of the organization so that everyone has objectives that can be directly linked to the organization's objectives.

It's here that I'm going to call bullshit.

In your organization, you might have truck drivers, factory workers, warehouse workers, etc. To try to define objectives for them that directly track to the organization's objectives is futile. Surely what you really need to know is how well they're doing what their job description says they should be doing? That description might include, for example, a warehouse worker that has to pick so many items per shift. So there's your real targets right in front of you. To try to create objectives for them that link to the business's EBITDA is surely ridiculous.[2] We all see managers every year go through the objective-setting process, that they know is worthless and requires enormous powers of creativity to work around the system. And when they're done, they never refer back to massively fudged objectives.

And don't get all uppity about it because of the apocryphal tale that gets quoted at us all the time, of the janitor at NASA who told JFK that his job was to put a man on the moon. Yeah, of course, that's a good thing. But it's different: that describes the ultimate goal/purpose of the organization. It does *not* describe a linkage to the no-doubt myriad of KPIs that NASA were managing against. If your organization makes stuff, you'd want your forklift drivers, packers and truck drivers to know that, ultimately, they're contributing to getting the right stuff, to the right place, at the right time. But that's the purpose of the organization and not the measure of whether they're doing their part to contribute to it. The forklift driver's measures will be about whether they showed up on time, respected the safety

---

[2] EBITDA – earnings before interest, taxes, depreciation and amortization.

policies and moved stuff around efficiently. Did the janitor at NASA clean more toilets, more often in order to get a man on the moon? Dunno. And if they did, did this get recognized in their annual appraisal? Did they have an objective of 'put a man on the moon?' If they did, they most certainly should have rejected it because it was entirely out of their control.

On the other hand, there might be people doing those jobs who want to develop their careers and would value being set 'objectives' that help them to grow, get spotted and get promoted. Well, that's very do-able too. The rail freight organization I mentioned earlier had exactly this challenge. Many of the train drivers and maintenance engineers were only interested in doing that job. They had no interest in career progression. However, others *did* want to move onwards and upwards. So in the annual performance appraisal system, we built in a mechanism by which these people could opt in or out of the objective-setting process. Those that opted in were set 'additional challenges' to help them to develop and stretch. Notice that we're still not going anywhere near the word 'objectives' to define this – we're keeping it real.

Since we've been calling out bullshit, let's also talk about annual appraisals. This is a topic for a different book/rant – but it's hard not to climb on to my soap box about it. The idea of reviewing someone's performance at the end of the year is total nonsense, isn't it? Imagine an elite sports team manager that has a player who turns up late to training, doesn't listen to the team talk before the match and doesn't contribute to the team performance when they're on the pitch. If the team manager waited until the season was over to give that person feedback, they'd be sacked, wouldn't they? And yet that's what we do through annual appraisals. Mad.

Is objective-setting and review taken seriously in your organization? If not, get serious. Because this whole creating a performance culture thing falls apart if you can't seriously tell whether people are doing a good job of the job you hired them to do and whether they're getting better at it year-on-year.

I'm not going to go into more detail about this here because there's enough information about this stuff out there already to fill 196 Olympic size swimming pools (I made that number up too).

My last word on this goes to my friend I mentioned earlier, who coaches Olympic and Paralympic athletes. He says that in his world of elite sport, the mantra is 'improve or retire'. Wouldn't it be great if everyone strove continuously to better themselves, technically, emotionally and existentially? If that were the case, we'd probably end up with far better politicians than we get saddled with now, far better parents, far better managers, far better employees, far better citizens of our communities. Sorry, I'll dismount my high horse now.

Performance management system to apply consequences

I'll describe why this is the silver bullet for culture change in the next chapter. For now, let's just deal with the tools you'll need to do this.

You have to have a robust performance management system that will do these things for you:

1. **Set 'task' performance goals**

   a. Pre-allocate mandatory objectives linked to corporate-level objectives

   b. Allow managers to set their own objectives in addition to the ones above

   c. Prompt managers to set objectives with their team members (but see point above about whether 'objectives' are the right thing)

   d. Prompt managers to review performance against objectives

   e. Capture performance against goals

   f. Collate data.

2. **Set behavioural performance goals** (against the required behaviours you've defined)

   a. Pre-allocate mandatory behavioural objectives linked to corporate-level cultural requirements

   b. Ask individuals to define who will complete their 360 questionnaire

   c. Send invitations to those 360 questionnaire completers (and reminders when they haven't done it)

   d. Capture performance against goals

   e. Collate data and generate a 360 report

   f. Allocate a coach for those who need it.

3. **Apply positive and negative consequences** (Don't forget – the next chapter will describe why this is the silver bullet for culture change.)

a. System prompts managers to have the next formal performance review with each member of their team

b. System generates automatic consequences for performance (positive and negative)

c. System allows managers to allocate their own discretionary positive and negative consequences

d. System raises a flag in HR when an under-performing person has an under-performing manager. This is because it's unlikely that an under-performing manager will have the skills and/or motivation to handle their under-performing team member themselves. HR can then step in

e. System tracks all progress for all individuals.

If you're lucky, you'll have a system that does all of this already. If not, it's a surprisingly easy thing to build. For example, using an application like SharePoint won't cost anywhere near as much as you think. And you've probably got people in-house who can do this.

My advice? Crack on. Now. You will *not* change your culture without it because everything hangs off being able to accurately measure performance (behavioural and task) and being able to apply consequences. Remember applying positive and negative consequences is the silver bullet to changing your culture rapidly. And you can't do that unless you can accurately measure performance. Get it? Got it? Good.

Chapter 8

Step 5 – Reward and Reprimand

STEP 1:
Define and Decree

the behavioural standards you expect of everyone

STEP 2:
Excite and Educate

everyone about how to embody and embed those standards

STEP 3:
Exert and Enable

performance by aligning your infrastructure

STEP 4:
Assess and Advise

people's performance against those standards

STEP 5:
Reward and Reprimand

positive and negative performance

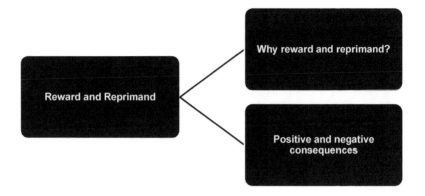

A gain, you might be thinking that 'reprimand' is a very strong word and is a bit mean and draconian. Perhaps you think this word is more suitable for naughty children in the playground. I disagree. I believe it's exactly the right word. If someone is under-performing, obviously yes, of course, give them feedback and try to find out why their performance is sub-standard. Particularly if they used to be a strong performer: is there a problem at home? Is there a problem at work? Have you promoted a square peg into a round hole? If their performance still doesn't improve, and you see no sign of them being even interested in improving their performance, why would you tolerate it?

Put it this way again: if you were the private owner of the business and you had to pay people out of your own pocket, would you tolerate under-performers? I've often asked Executive Teams: 'If I were to give you a piece of paper and a pen and lock the door, could you write down the names of people who've been under-performing for a while?' They always say 'yes'. To which of course I reply: 'Well, what are you going to do about it?!' Although, in my head, I'm screaming 'aaaaagggghhhhhh!!!!!'

Small businesses wouldn't tolerate under-performance for long because they're almost immediately able to see the impact on the bottom line. But there's something about large organizations which means that dead wood is tolerated for far longer. And indeed, as we all know, in some cases, dead wood floats.

Why reward and reprimand?

Doing this is the silver bullet. This *will* change your culture fast if you do it properly. Adapting your performance management system so that good things happen if you perform, and zero good things, and even bad things, happen if you don't perform, serves to reinforce the required behaviours. This is a reinforcement that the organization is serious, and a reinforcement of the need to use the required behaviours every day.

I'll say it again: this is what will drive rapid culture change. I reckon I could change everyone's behaviour overnight. If I said to them go home now and come back tomorrow using the required behaviours or you won't get paid, that would certainly focus their attention. Of course, I couldn't do that because a) it doesn't give anyone the chance to change, develop and grow; and b) I'd find myself in court fighting a Class Action suit. But you see my point? If you say that behavioural performance is really, really important but then you don't measure or reward behavioural performance, nothing will change. Or at least, it won't change fast enough.

Despite this, I've worked with many Executive Teams who understand, and agree with, the principle. And then we get to the point in the culture change programme where we've 1) Defined and Decreed the behavioural standards expected of everyone; 2) Excited and Educated them about what the target culture can do for us and educated them in how to live those behaviours; 3) Exerted and Enabled them to perform; 4) Assessed and Advised them about their current performance and where they need to make changes. And now the rubber has hit the proverbial: the Executive Team now need to consider negative consequences for under-performers who have been given the feedback, but who show no sign of being either willing or able (or both) to improve. The Executive Team initially agreed with the principle of applying negative consequences but often, at this point, I've found that they get a bit squeamish about it. Obfuscating to avoid the difficult decisions – and often going through a 'cuddle cycle' – we have a problem, we need to do something about it, actually it's not as bad as we thought, so we really don't need to do anything. A lovely group hug. But I remind them that the people who have to work alongside these under-performers will be liberated by your decision to remove the under-performers *and* will judge you harshly if you don't deal with them.

Positive and negative consequences

Let's get stuck into what the consequences might be. First, let's start by making sure we're clear about the difference between recognition and reward. Rewards are conditional and often transactional – you achieved this, so we're giving you that. You're meeting/exceeding all of your goals, so we want to retain you and progress you in the organization. Recognitions are appreciations and therefore more relational. In your organization, you might have something like 'values thank you cards' where you send someone a thank you for living up to one of the values. A lot of people really like them. But note, you might get ten of these in a week, but still not have the full task and behavioural skill set to progress in the organization.

What might the positive and negative consequences be? The following are the outputs of a workshop I ran recently in an organization to help them define their positive and negative consequences.

Positive, automated (by the performance management system) REWARD consequences:

- Financial rewards (team and personal)
- Access to additional growth and development opportunities (including coaching)
- Entry into the talent pool and prioritization for career progression
- Special project opportunities
- Earned autonomy
- Mentoring from local businesses
- Salary sacrifice add-ons

Positive, manager-discretion RECOGNITION items:

- Annual award ceremony nominations
- Additional annual leave day

- 'A star works in this department' sign
- Prize draw entry
- Staff lottery
- Thank you cards
- Pin badges/mugs
- Afternoon tea with the CEO/Chair
- Recognition certificate
- Membership to local attractions
- Parking space
- Vouchers for canteen or discounts with local organizations

Negative, automated (by the performance management system) REWARD consequences:

- Absence of positive consequences (e.g. don't get pay increment)
- Removal of earned autonomy/increased monitoring
- Development limited to role development rather than career development
- Placed on an HR Performance Improvement Plan
- Moving people backwards down the pay increment scale
- Turnaround team put in place

Notice how the recognition items might reinforce the required behaviours but they do nothing about progressing the individual. They're good and have a place, but the reward items are far, far, far more important in terms of continuously improving performance in your organization. And, by the way, you know those succession plan issues you have? This is the cure.

Obviously, some of those (particularly the recognition items) won't necessarily work in your organization. You have to decide what works best for you. But I'd be really surprised if any of the negative consequences *didn't* apply in your organization.

You don't have to change attitudes first

One of the things that will slow your culture change endeavours down is if you plan to change attitudes before behaviour. Many argue that you have to change the attitude that drives behaviour in order to change the behaviour. I completely disagree. Let's say my kid is being bullied by another kid at school because the bully has an attitude (that they've learned from somewhere) that asserting your own strength over another person is OK. I don't really care right now about changing their underpinning attitude. I just want them to stop hitting my kid. We can sort their attitude out later. Or if someone says something racist, homophobic, misogynist or transphobic, we can sit them down and sort out their vile attitude later – but for now, just stop behaving like an egregious human being.

We're all driven by our attitudes. Here's proof. Many people speed on the motorway. They know that the speed limit is there to keep everyone safe. But we speed because our attitude is that we think we're safe drivers; the road is dry and it's OK for us to speed. And as we're cruising along at about 80mph, we see a police car parked in a lay-by. So we slow down. The presence of the police officer has compelled us to behave differently. What do we do next? Check the rear-view mirror, police officer hasn't budged, so foot on the gas and off we go again – because our underpinning attitude is that it's OK for us to speed. The presence of the police officer changed our behaviour but not our underpinning attitude. I think you'd agree that it would take a lot to change our attitude to speeding. Ever been on one of those four-hour speed awareness courses? Hour after hour of genuinely compelling information about how speeding costs lives. Maybe you drove all the way home at the speed limit. (Maybe you didn't.) But how long was it before you were driving above the speed limit again?

In other words, you can change people's behaviour without having to change their underlying attitudes. The trick is to ensure that changes to behaviour are lasting rather than fleeting as in the motorway example. That's what applying positive and negative consequences does for you. It reinforces, and in some ways compels, the behaviours you want.

There are two tricks here:

1. Invest as much as you can in step 2: Excite and Educate. Obviously, if people are excited about the possibilities that would emerge from behaviour change (individual and collective) and educated about what this means in practice, they're more likely to change their attitudes.
2. Avoid fleeting behaviour change – as if it were a tick-box exercise that will soon go away – by reinforcing positive and negative performance through your performance management system.

I know what you're thinking… you're thinking that we don't want to have to police the use of our required behaviours. That's just negative. Correct. So put it this way: what if driving at the speed limit for a whole year meant you were given £5,000, i.e. a positive consequence? Positive consequences are just as important as negative consequences.

PART 3

Making it stick
and evolve

Chapter 9

Leading and driving culture change

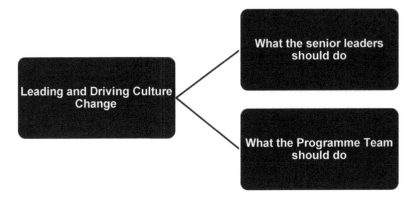

Leading rapid culture change needs a Senior Leadership Team and Programme Team that are committed, focussed and role modelling the required behaviours, who are willing and able to remove obstacles and capitalize on enablers, can be out in the organization making change happen and who have the skills to engage the workforce consistently and inspirationally.

Does that sound like a tall order? Well, the whole culture change effort starts with getting your senior leader ducks in a row and needs a Programme Team that is willing to battle the old culture in order to implement the new one.

What the senior leaders should do

Don't even think about trying to get the rest of the organization to use the required behaviours if your senior leaders aren't living them. This might mean getting rid of a few and will definitely involve serious commitment to personal development.

Here's a list of things the Senior Leadership Team must do in order to deliver rapid change. What do I mean by 'senior'? Well, it's definitely every single one of the Executive Team. It's definitely all of their Direct Reports. And it's probably all of *their* Direct Reports. If you can go deeper into the leadership population then so much the better.

1. **Don't collude with the old culture**. I've described that the biggest impediment to the introduction of a new culture is the old culture. For example, let's say that culturally, you're aiming to move at greater pace, collaborate optimally and become less risk adverse. But you find that your programme steering committee is unwilling to make difficult decisions (risk adverse), meets only once a month to make those decisions (slow) and either engages too many or too few stakeholders (sub-optimal collaboration). This is the old culture getting in the way of the new culture. Everything you do from project initiation needs to be pressure tested against the target culture – are we doing everything in alignment with our culture aspirations?

2. **Move at speed to build momentum**. It's the golden rule for all transformation programmes. A change programme must move at speed. Moving at speed drives

momentum. And momentum creates a snowball effect of people engaging and delivering. It's about creating a bow-wave of change that becomes utterly irresistible.

Moving at speed has two key component parts:

a. How you make decisions.

Define who has decision-making authority and set up processes and decision-making forums that allow them to make decisions. Use the bureaucracy busting process I've described and set up the Change Council I've outlined. Ditherers and procrastinators should either not be included in decision-making or give them the feedback that they dither and coach them to move more rapidly. There's always a reason why people don't move at speed, for example they might be scared of making the wrong decision; they might not have access to all of the data needed to make a high-quality decision; they don't have the delegated authority to make those decisions; their boss won't let them make the decisions; they're so overwhelmed with other work that this sits low down on the to-do list. What do you do about them? Easy – find out why! And then help them to change. See the next chapter for more information about coaching (Chapter 10).

b. Executing decisions.

Hold people to account. Failure to deliver (without good reason) should not be tolerated.

Moving at speed is the best tool you have to help you break through the treacle of the old culture into the new way of performing. Do not underestimate the power of the old culture to draw people back into doing things in the same old ways. Habits are just that – habitual. You don't even notice them. And they're hard to break.

3. **Role model**. The senior leaders have to be in the organization every day, living the behaviours, calling out the bad behaviours when they see them and constantly reinforcing the value of performing in the new, different way. I recently read that you have to say something about 65 times in order for it to sink in. (That certainly seems to be the case with getting my kids to put their shoes away.)

   For this to work, first you have to focus hard on self-development. In other words, you must get your senior leadership ducks in a row before going out into the rest of the organization. Later on, I describe the scheduling of your culture interventions. It shows that the top-down, middle-out and bottom-up elements should be staggered. Starting with the most senior people: people mostly look around them for examples of how to behave. However, if they look up and see any inconsistencies, they'll leap on it while pointing vigorously and declaring, 'see, I told you they didn't mean it.'

   Part of this is also about making some big decisions: what do you do with those Brilliant Jerks that we talked about earlier? Those people who are technically superb but behaviourally dreadful and beyond repair? The answer is simple. You have to part ways. It's not (necessarily) that they're bad people, it's just that they can't do what you're asking them to do. And even worse, one under-performing senior person will have a negative multiplier effect on potentially dozens or even hundreds of other people.

4. **Inspire**. Your senior leaders need to be inspirational. Let's be clear first what that doesn't mean. It doesn't mean leaping onto the table in the canteen and full-throatedly delivering a St Crispian's Day-type speech: 'We few, we happy few, we band of brothers...'. Although if you want to, go for it, do it. Inspiration can be very quiet too. But to do it, there's one essential thing that the leaders have to do: they have to leave their ego behind. It's not about them. It's about the people who spend most of their waking hours working for them. It's about engaging them by speaking honestly, no spin, no bullshit, talking through the negatives and helping them to see the positives. It's about sharing the pain and sharing the good stuff. People can smell manipulation from about 100 metres away and they will reject what you're saying as corporate bollocks rather than real, passionate ideas and direction.

    Egos have no place here. The bigger the ego the less space there is for anyone else. The people who get this right, in all aspects of life, fill a room without demanding space.

    So here's the summary of what you need to do to inspire: have real conversations with people. Er, that's it. It's as simple as that. The more time leaders spend having straight, positively-intended conversations with people, the faster your organization will change. Trust builds very rapidly in the sunshine of honesty. Also, people expect to be involved rather than be done to. So if that expectation is not met, they won't engage. The principle is that we take far better care of something that we feel belongs to us than something that's not ours.

You can't fudge this by trying to show you care about them by putting ping pong tables in the office. (In fact, there's evidence to suggest that Millennial males would rather have more paternity leave than ping pong tables and free fizzy drinks.)[1] It's about getting personal, it's about really, really (really) listening and it's about creating the band of brothers and sisters that Henry V was banging on about.

5. **Make some changes**. The faster the senior leaders start dealing with the treacle-y crap that gets in everyone's way, and the faster they start dealing with under-performers and nurturing star performers, and the faster that their own performance changes to reflect the required behaviours, the faster everyone else will change. Remember the monkey's tale at the beginning of this book? If the biggest obstacle to the introduction of a new culture is the old culture, it's also true that the biggest enabler of the introduction of a new culture is

---

[1] There are lots of articles that demonstrate this through surveys. Here's one: https://qbeeurope.com/news-and-events/press-releases/british-men-and-women-want-paternity-leave-to-double-workers-attitudes-and-expectations-shift/ (accessed February 2024).

behaving in the new culture way. Does that sound like I've just reduced something very complex to something completely facile? I know it sounds like it, but I haven't. You don't believe that people will just do what other people do? Well, when you need to take a break, search for some old *Candid Camera* footage on the internet. In one of the shows, they put four men in a lift. When another man gets in and the doors shut, the four original men all simultaneously turn 90 degrees to the right. The new man looks slightly baffled, but after literally about five seconds, he turns too. And then the four turn a further 90 degrees. New man follows. In another scene, the four men get into the lift to join a man who's already standing in there. They all, as one, turn to face the rear of the lift. (No one faces backwards in a lift do they?) The original man looks a bit unsettled... and then turns to face the back of the lift.

I know it seems that the message is that we have the backbone of an octopus after two bottles of Prosecco. But the moral of this story is this: we like to fit in. We adapt to fit our surroundings. We can choose not to interpret this as weakness. Instead, we can interpret this as an openness to new ideas and ways of doing things. Some don't of course. And they're the ones that need extra feedback and coaching.

I guarantee that your culture will change at an exponential pace when you get a bow-wave effect from your senior leaders quickly adopting the new required behaviours.

What the Programme Team should do

None of this will happen without a dedicated team of people planning and executing the plan. I've got two 'by the ways' here.

'By the way' number 1

The programme should not be led by HR. As I've said before, the idea that the team that knows most about other people in the organization is a support function (and therefore, by definition, one step removed from day-to-day operations) is complete insanity. The Programme Team might have a representative or two from HR (particularly when it comes to aligning the people management practices that I talked about earlier) but most of them should come from operational roles. And led by a very senior person. Because a senior person lends credibility and serves as a built-in tool to remove obstacles and challenge other senior people.

'By the way' number 2

The members of the Programme Team have to be true 'multipliers' – technically excellent and behaviourally brilliant. I mention this because far too often I've seen people being carelessly put into programme teams 'who can be spared'. In other words, they're no good at their day job so they're moved out of the way… into a strategically vital programme. Hmmmm.

Here's a list of things the Programme Team *must* do:

1. **Maximize, don't minimize**. At all times think about the art of the possible. Don't revert to old ways of doing

things or what you've seen done before. Even if some of those things worked, think about what *more* you could do. Posters, values thank you cards, a generic leadership development programme, etc. might all sound good in themselves, but if added together, are they going to rapidly change the culture?

You should make 'start with the art of the possible' your mantra – call it one of your programme guiding principles, perhaps. This allows you to ward off the minimizers who have a reductive mindset. By the way, let's not judge them for that. Often, the minimizers I've met are operating out of fear. They fear making a mistake because that's the culture of the place and therefore don't want to take what they consider to be 'risks'. Other minimizers I've encountered are operating from a place of overwhelm. They've got so much going on that they can't conceive of being able to take on any more work. Again, this is often a function of the culture of the organization.

2. **Plan meticulously**. There's no excuse for making it up as you go along. Or even having a broad idea of what's going to be done. Plans should drill down to even the tiniest of tasks like booking rooms and buying flipchart paper. Meticulous planning also includes knowing your budget right from the start so that you know exactly what you can and can't do. I've seen too many culture change programmes not just fail but leave the organization worse off than it was before because hopes were raised and then dashed because the Programme

Team couldn't ultimately deliver what they promised. Often because budget wasn't made available.

3. **Execute the plan lucidly, unwaveringly and seamlessly**. This means:

   a. Lucidly = clearly.
   b. Unwaveringly = doing the tough stuff and not being diverted by people using old behaviours.
   c. Seamlessly = all moving parts joined up and working like an aerobatic display team.

4. **Measure culture change progress**. Define your goals at the start. Define how you're going to measure progress and adjust plans if you're not delivering against targets. There are three levels of measure:

   a. *Input measures*: did we do what we said we'd do? On time, on budget and on quality?

      Measure these things using the usual programme management methods.

   b. *Output measures*: did we produce what we said we'd deliver?

      For example, all the Senior Leadership Team coaching sessions happened, everyone took up their one-to-one coaching opportunities, all the middle-out workshops happened.

      Measure this by rigorous reporting against the plan. You should be evaluating the quality of what you produce not whether you produced it (this is covered in input measures). To understand the quality of what you've produced, you should be asking people. Make it a standard practice that after every single intervention, you ask for direct feedback. This must include specifically asking what could have been better – directly challenging them to challenge you.

c. *Outcome measures*: what changed?

These are the 'so what' measures: OK, so we've produced all the outputs, on time, etc., but has the culture changed? There are two sets of data you should collect here:

i. Qualitative data via a barometer group

I always like to set up a group of about 20 to 30 people to provide qualitative data. The number of people will, of course, vary based on the size of the organization – but you must ensure you have a group who represent a true diagonal slice through the organization (grades and functions). I get them together about once a month to ask the same three questions:

- What are people saying about the changes?
- What are people doing differently?
- What's not working? (At all, or not fast enough.)

This group gives you access to the jungle drums. Straight information about how the programme is going. In other words, they give you a barometer reading of how the organization is feeling.

You listen, you act and you report back what you've changed in your plans at the next session.

Plus it has the major bonus effect that if you really listen with humility and act with ambition, you now have about 30 people who will go out into the organization and tell everyone what a cracking programme this is. Or put more professionally, they'll tell everyone that you're serious... as opposed to all of the previous change programmes that have had a big, trumpeted fanfare launch, followed by tumbleweed blowing through all of those meeting rooms with lovely new bean bags and cool slogans on the walls.

By the way, don't confuse this group with 'change agents'. I'm never quite sure what change agents are. Does anyone know? It's almost become an unspoken law that change programmes must have change agents. But I've rarely seen an organization actually change because of its network of change agents. Some, maybe. Most, no.

ii. Quantitative data – via baseline and on-going pulse surveys

This is really simple. Take your culture imperatives and ask, in a survey, how much of each they see today. Four questions. That's it. The small number of questions will increase your chances of people responding to the survey. If you have a lot of people in your organization who are 'unwired', i.e. they don't spend much time in front of a computer screen, think about using other methods to collect this data, for example put a flipchart by the entrance/exit door and ask people to give their ratings.

Now you have your baseline. Which means that you can repeat this process on a monthly or quarterly basis to see how much things are changing. And if they're not changing, or not changing as fast as they should, find out why (talk to people!!!) and adjust plans accordingly.

Of course, the ultimate goal of changing your culture is to have an impact on the performance of the business. This impact is very difficult to measure – so many other things might have contributed to business performance going up or down. Nonetheless, the Executive Team should be talking about the impact of culture on performance as part of their business performance review meetings. They will now have an instinctive sense of whether the culture is helping or hindering productivity, quality and service levels.

Let's be clear: you must start by defining outcome measures. From these you can determine what outputs you need to deliver, and from these you can decide the inputs you need to generate those outputs. Too many programmes start with input measures – which, given what I've just said, makes no sense. *And* I've seen many, many, many multi-million pound programmes that don't have a clearly articulated statement of the outcomes (benefits) that will accrue from the programme: 'So we've spent £3.5m on a new enterprise-wide system… what was it for again?' Would you spend your money like this? Unless you have a gambling habit, you would not.

If you're doing your job well and engaging staff fully, they *will* ask you how you're going to measure success. If you don't have the answers, throw a sicky on the day you know you're going to get asked. There's no excuse for not knowing this at the start.

5. Effortful communication

- **Communicate**. Listen, act, listen, act, listen, act… repeat until successful. Remember that the job is to *manage* resistance not *remove* resistance. They're probably resisting because you've got something wrong, you're not really listening or you're not applying the right effort to the right things.

- **Build a proactive communications plan**. Programme communications are not about spewing out broadcast emails to all staff every so often. Or when you realize you haven't communicated for a while. It's about creating a plan that delivers specific messages to specific groups of people at specific points in time using specific communications media. This is a labour-intensive task and needs dedicated resources. People need to know what's being changed and when. And then they need to know when things have changed. Open and transparent communications allow people to trust that you're doing what they know needs to be done. Don't be afraid to say when you get something wrong and shout it loud when things go right. No spin, just the truth. Basically, do the exact opposite of politicians. Here's some examples of things I've done to communicate, which in themselves state that things are different by not resorting to the usual, dull, communication methods, for example a broadcast email to everyone (that they don't read) telling them what's happening in the project, or the monthly newsletter (that people read largely to look for photos of people they know):

➢ *Culture blueprint.* A clear statement of where we are now culturally, why we need to change and what we need to change into. Produced in both digital and hard-copy formats (for those who don't work with laptops all day). Written in every day English – not corporate speak. Written with only one or two sentences (or even one or two words) per page to make it more likely that the emphatic nature of the writing encourages people to turn the pages.

➢ *TV broadcast.* During Covid lockdown, we capitalized on having a captive audience at home, by setting up a TV studio in a hotel ballroom and broadcasting to all staff simultaneously (the organization were key workers, so a small number of us were allowed out to do this). The day was full of interesting content, presented by interesting people. We sent a package to everyone's homes in advance that included materials they'd need to have at hand during the broadcast, lunch and snacks to keep them going through the day. The best part was the 'chat' function on the online viewing portal that allowed everyone to throw their thoughts in throughout the day. We had a team of people who were monitoring the chat and feeding me key points into my car piece. I was able to respond 'live', including when I was interviewing the CEO, being able to say 'people in the chat are asking why they should believe you. They've heard all this before. What would you say to them?'

➢ *CEO honest updates.* We asked the CEO to talk honestly in their monthly global town hall meetings to describe what they and their Executive Team are getting out of the team coaching process. Honestly describing the challenges they've faced and what they've tried to change, what they've succeeded in and what hasn't worked yet.

➢ *Challenge and support.* The Programme Team must be willing and able to challenge. Hard. They've got to be able to challenge the nay-sayers; they've got to be able to challenge the speed of decision-making; they've got to be able to challenge when they hear the sound of the 'too difficult' stuff being swept quietly under the front door mat. Read Chapter 10 for much more insight about this and the tools to do it effectively.

Chapter 10

Caring candour... drives continuous culture evolution

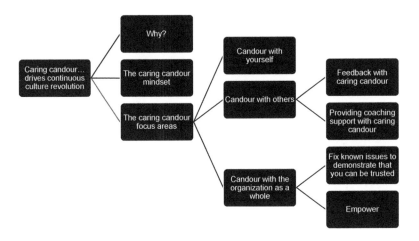

Why?

'Can I be honest...?' No. I want you to lie to me.

Why do so many people start a sentence with that phrase? Of course I want you to be honest! Why would you even think it was worth wasting oxygen suggesting that I would want anything other than that?

Well, I suppose it's because a lot of people think that you can't speak the whole truth because it's not very nice. It's not kind. It's not friendly.

In fact, I would argue that to sit in a meeting (or at a kitchen table), mentally disagreeing with what someone is saying, and perhaps even seeing risks associated with it, and *not* saying anything is very *un*kind and *un*friendly.

And that's why caring candour is critical:

to be candid because you genuinely care about the outcome.

This chapter describes the absolute imperative to be caringly candid when driving culture change and then driving continuous culture evolution and performance improvement when the new culture has bedded-in. Your culture should continue to evolve as business performance grows, competitors' performance changes and market conditions change.

I worked in a healthcare organization a while ago. At the time, we defined a culture imperative of 'we do what we say we'll do.' A year later, this had progressed so much that people wondered why they even needed to talk about it in the first place... 'of course we do what we say we'll do!' This culture imperative evolved into 'we always do what our customers need us to do.' And another year later, mission accomplished, this evolved into 'we focus on what our customers will need in the future.'

Continuous culture growth and improvement is essential. Culture change shouldn't be thought of as a one-off exercise. Caring candour is the magic key that unlocks continuous improvement. Why? Because speaking the truth is faster, enables everyone to contribute – not just the HiPPO (the Highest Paid Person's Opinion) and removes all constraints on ideas and opportunities – at the same time as naming and speedily managing risks. I call it a 'magic' key because when you start practising caring candour, it will feel like someone has waved a magic wand. Everything changes. The horizon seems to shift from near to far, collaboration becomes incredibly productive and joy returns. And why is it important that joy returns? Because joy is a lubricant that makes everything feel simpler and faster to do. At the time of writing, I'm working with an excellent CEO. At the beginning of the culture change endeavours they said: 'Our people are incredibly dedicated, but we rely too much on goodwill. We've got to bring back the joy.' They get it.

My intention when writing this book was to be entirely candid. My aim was to deliver key messages clearly and directly. As I said at the beginning of the book, I imagine that some readers might have found the straight-talking a little uncomfortable. However, what would be the point in being equivocal, what would be the point in not speaking the truth when my sole intention was to support and help? I could have applied window dressing to a number of my assertions: 'Perhaps you might like to try this' or 'Is it OK if I play devil's advocate for a moment?' But how can you trust that I'm on top of my subject when I don't honestly state what I believe to be true? Which doesn't mean I'm not open to new ways of thinking. I update my thinking and tools all the time on the basis of my own and others' learning.

If what I'm trying to do is help, then there's no point in pulling my punches. And yet that it is what many people do. At work. With their partner. With their friends. With their kids. They do this because of some misplaced sense that to speak the truth would be hurtful or unkind or unfriendly. Yes, of course it would be horrible if your intention was to belittle them, or big-up your ego, or angrily assert your own position. But no, it definitely wouldn't be hurtful, unkind or unfriendly if you have a positive, caring intent, i.e. your intention in being candid is to make things better.

By the way – because I know where your brain might have just gone – that doesn't mean those people who can be blunt to the point of rude. Caring candour means speaking the truth in a way that makes clear your positive intent. If you're at work, this means being a respectful, benevolent manager or colleague. At home, this means your honest thoughts come from a place of love and kindness.

I just slipped in the word 'benevolent' there. Some think benevolence is soft, meek and even insipid. But actually, benevolence means being compassionate, humane and gracious. Surely wonderful leadership or teammate qualities. You can be all of those things while being candid. In fact, I would argue that you can't be compassionate, humane and gracious *unless* you're candid; otherwise, to some extent or other, you're faking it.

For the conflict-avoidant reader, I hope this chapter will be a game-changer. For those who often feel unheard, I hope this will help you increase your personal power and impact. For those who find it difficult to speak truth to power, I hope this will encourage and help. For those who shy away from giving feedback (downwards, sideways or upwards), my intention is that this will provide an instruction manual.

Honestly, it's taken me a long time to even learn the importance of caring candour in life. It's an active decision to learn how to do it. And I'm definitely still a work in progress. I have to catch myself pulling a punch with clients, being defensive with my wife and window dressing a response because I think being 'nice' will protect the recipient.

I was lucky. I married an extremely talented psychotherapist and Executive Coach. She's helped me to understand where my conflict avoidance came from. Not so that I could wallow in the trauma of various events in my life, but to help me understand what causes me to behave the way I do. This helped me to understand why I've constructed myself the way I have and then *change*. Re-build, re-define, choose something different, learn different patterns of behaviour and then *be* that person. Am I advocating that everyone has a therapist or coach? Yes. Yes I am. If you're at all interested in truly being the best version of yourself, then yes. Get a coach. If you're truly interested in being the best manager, partner, parent or friend you can be, get a coach.

My cousin Dave is a builder. He said something truly brilliant to me a few years ago. You need to read this in a wrong side of the tracks, East End of London, cockney accent: 'Andrew, I go to the gym to exercise my body, I go to my coach to exercise my mind.' No need to say any more. Unless you didn't read it in a cockney accent, in which case read it again in that voice, and it sounds even better.

That's why when people start a sentence with 'can I be honest...?' I often think 'I don't know... can you?'

Noel Coward wrote: 'It's discouraging to think how many people are shocked by honesty and how few by deceit.'

This is an interesting reflection because I suspect that many people would not describe pulling punches or avoiding conflict as 'deceit'. But think of it this way, the word we use for not telling the truth is 'lying'. And none of us would like to think of ourselves as liars. But definitionally, when we're not engaging in caring candour, we are being deceitful. We are actively trying to deceive others about our true thoughts, opinions and feelings. We're actually… lying.

What does this mean for driving culture change?

- Culture change – or any transformation effort – simply won't work unless we're truly candid about what's working, what's not working and about ideas we've had to improve performance. Even if we fear we might hurt someone's feelings.

- We must encourage and enable everyone in the organization to voice their thoughts candidly. How else do we expose the truth about what's really going on, so that we can do something about it? How else do we harness the full horsepower of our people's brains?

- People will not engage in sustaining the new culture nor continue to evolve it if they feel unheard. If they feel that they have true agency to continuously look for faster, better, cheaper, safer ways of doing things, then you have a real continuous improvement environment (which has a double benefit, by the way, because it means you don't have to spend lots of money on training people to be six sigma yellow belts, who might join the long list of lean acolytes in organizations that do nothing with their new skills and therefore achieve nothing because no one's freaking listening).

Let's talk about how to 'do' caring candour. There's no point talking about theory, we've got to get stuck into the practical stuff.

All of this is predicated on the notion of generating positive conflict through caring candour. Engaging with others in this way creates productive tension. The tension is about giving birth to new ideas and new ways of looking at things, it's about building on others' ideas to get better results and it's about getting to the guts of what's really going on so that you either fix the problem or capitalize on the opportunity.

Remember the spectrum of conflict we looked at earlier?

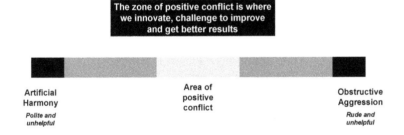

Politely 'agreeing' when you don't actually agree or getting pointy fingered, angry and shouty when you don't agree, will not move the situation forward. So let's look at how to encourage everyone to operate in the zone of positive conflict through caring candour.

First, the caring candour mindset and then some caring candour focus areas.

The caring candour mindset

There are some fundamentals about the way we think that need to be addressed in order to be caringly candid:

- **No window dressing.** Don't start sentences with things like, 'can I just play devil's advocate' or 'you know me, I like to question things' or 'do you mind if I throw a thought in?' This is just window dressing. If you have something to say, just say it. Everyone knows that your window dressing is just preamble to what you're going to say, so why not just get on with it?

  If you were to observe my friend and colleague Andy and I working together, you might think we didn't like each other because there is zero window dressing. You might hear one of us saying 'that won't work because…' or 'that idea is OK, but it would be better if we…'. We don't have the time or inclination to beat around the bush. We always operate on the principle of positive conflict, i.e. challenges are made to get a better result. By the way, you won't ever hear us saying things like 'that's stupid' or 'you always miss the point.' These are personal and offensive. We focus on the issue not the person. We also have a rule that we can challenge the challenge. We don't have to just accept a challenge. That would be daft. If we don't agree, we say so – again on the basis of wanting to get the best possible result. If you spot that the debate is getting circular and not getting anywhere, point it out and either find a solution that both parties can accept or commit to coming back to it after further thought.

- **No complaint without recommendation**. Have a zero-tolerance policy for complaints without recommendations. A synonym for complaining without a recommendation is 'whingeing'. If you hear someone issue a complaint, immediately follow it up with 'and what's your recommendation?' If they don't have one, ask them to go away and think about it... and don't complain without a recommendation again. Pretty quickly, this becomes a modus operandi across the team.

- **Avoid the fundamental attribution error**. Fundamental attribution error is a cognitive bias that encourages us to think that people behave in a certain way because of *who* they are rather than the *situation* they're in. For example, we might judge someone harshly for being late. We might label them as 'lazy'. But in fact, they might be late because they're taking care of a sick parent on the way to work every day. Caring candour is not possible when you're busy making assumptions and then forming judgements. Assumptions and judgements are likely to make us focus on the person rather than the situation. The person might turn out to be at fault, but you mustn't start with this premise. Human beings are extremely good at forming judgements. It's a survival skill: we need to quickly assess our surroundings and decide on a course of action. To demonstrate this, I'll sometimes ask a workshop group some questions about me. Let's say they've known me for only about an hour, but I ask them to tell me how I like my coffee, what kind of car I drive, what kind of home I live in, whether I have kids, etc. They initially squirm and tell me that they can't possibly know. I reply by saying that of course they can't *know*... but what do you think? Incredibly quickly they're able to generate answers. Their answers are based on assumptions that turn rapidly into judgements. They might tell me that I drive a ten-year-old family saloon. If I then tell them I drive a Ferrari, I can almost see their brains changing gears as they alter their assumptions and judgements about me. Many of us do this. It's a cognitive strategy for rapidly trying to make sense of the world. It doesn't make us bad people. However, real candour can't be based on assumptions. Real candour is based on truth and seeks the truth. The truth does not lie in assumptions and judgements. Training ourselves to spot when we're falling prey to the fundamental attribution error is very important.

- **Avoid the cuddle cycle**. This is where the group decides there's a problem, then slowly agrees that it's not so bad after all and then concludes that everything is OK. A group cuddle. You can only decide that the problem doesn't require attention after candid conversation. I often see teams work in this way when there's a dawning realization that if they were to acknowledge this as a problem, there's going to be a ton of extra work on their desk within the hour. It's like noticing your washing machine has a leak and then deciding that it's only a small leak, so no need to do anything other than put a towel on the floor. Is it actually a 'small' leak or are you trying to talk yourself out of having to pull the machine out, look up on YouTube how to diagnose the source of the leak, get your tools out… and, in my case, ultimately giving up and calling a plumber?

- **Own your own shit**. Owning your own shit means taking 100% responsibility for all of the relationships in your life. Not owning your shit means blaming others for how you feel and for any of the poor experiences you have. We all know people with this victim mentality. Nothing is their fault, it's always other people or other circumstances that have got in their way. Caring candour just can't work if you're not taking full responsibility for your part in any dispute, problem or difficult discussion.

The caring candour focus areas

I'm now going to talk about three areas where caring candour needs to be focussed:

1. Candour with yourself
2. Candour with others
3. Candour with the organization as a whole

Caring candour focus area 1: Candour with yourself

There are stacks of stuff we could look at it here, but let's focus on two critical elements of being candid with yourself:

1. **Embrace your emotions**. We learn very quickly that emotions are not acceptable at work. Things are definitely moving in the direction with many organizations trying to place emphasis on well-being. But that's only

part of the story – the part where we're feeling in a dark place and need support. The biggest part of embracing our emotions is to recognize that we're emotional creatures. And our emotions drive our thinking. And our thinking drives our actions.

We need to fully understand our emotions: if you're not candid with yourself about your emotions and where they come from, we cannot be fully in control ourselves. Our emotions are running the show. Think of someone who prides themself on being very rational. They don't show their emotions. They have big decisions to make and live in an almost constant state of anxiety. They don't show this or talk about it with their colleagues because they think it might make them look weak. Missing the opportunity to share with others that might be feeling the same or similar. Instead, they present a front of being cool, calm and collected. But the anxiety emotions drive their thoughts and actions so that they always choose the safe decision.

We talk about Emotional Intelligence (EI) as if we fully understand it. Most people seem to think that EI is about the social skills and empathy part of Goleman's model. What they seem to miss is the other part of his model which is all about understanding what's going on inside us and developing the skills to live with, manage and regulate those emotions appropriately.

What this boils down to is that we have to use candour to challenge ourselves just as much as we need to use it to challenge others. In fact, the combo of the two is incredibly effective: understanding yourself so that you can engage optimally with others.

2. **Being open not defensive**. Many of us will get defensive in the face of a challenge. I said this to a group recently and someone folded his arms and said, 'I don't.' Hmmm.

    Being open and non-defensive requires an ability to be humble. Being humble means having the humility to accept that someone else's view is better than yours. The flipside to this is feeling the joy – genuine joy – of working with people who make your ideas better or who help the team get a better result. You know that feeling of doing the first draft of a document and sending it off to others to review? Even though you know you've done the hard yards starting with a blank sheet of paper, even though you know that the editing process is now easier because of the graft you've put it in, there's still that buttock-clenching moment of opening the email with someone else's critique of your work. Think about the emotions you feel in that moment: irritation, anger, frustration, self-doubt, imposter syndrome. None of those feelings are positive, and therefore none of them are productive. Imagine instead, clicking that email with a smile on your face while thinking, 'oh good, this will get my 90% document to 100%.' I know. That's not easy. But it is possible. It means you have to re-train your brain to burrow down different neural pathways. And like all habits, they can be broken and new ones learned. You've just got to want to do it.

    Here's proof that it can be done: remove your watch and put it on your other wrist. The first thing you'll notice is that you're not as good at securing the watch to your wrist using your other hand. Now you'll notice that your watch feels weird on your other wrist. When you next look at your watch, you'll tut as you realize you've raised the wrong arm. And most of you will do this fewer than four times before you remove your watch and put it back where it belongs. That's habit. Changing habits feels weird and uncomfortable and even annoying. But let's say you stuck with it. How long would it take before you got used to it? Probably not very long. And what if there was an incentive to keep it there all week – someone gives you £1,000 for persisting. Now you feel the desire to change your habit. In other words, when we understand that there's a benefit to changing our habits, we're exponentially more likely to change them. And that's the place you have to get your head to: I want to change my response to being challenged because it's better for me and it's better for others.

Here's a self-coaching process that will help you shift from defensive to open:

I'm going to break that model down. But first let's recognize the importance of self-coaching in this scenario. If others aren't operating in the zone of positive conflict, they're unlikely to give you helpful feedback to hope you manage your defensive responses. The obstructive aggressors we talked about in Chapter 5 will just do more harrumphing and talk louder. The artificial harmonists will say nothing. The best source of information about what's going on for you and how you should respond is *you*. You literally know more about it than anyone else because it's all going on in your head. Self-coaching is the best way to change the defensive habit into an open one.

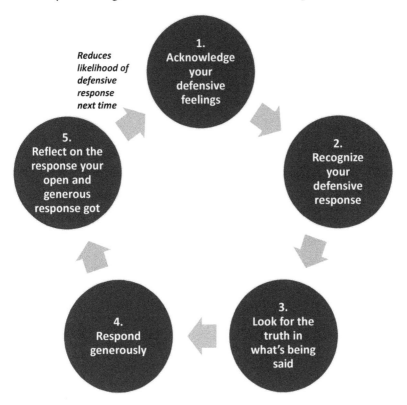

1. **Acknowledge your defensive feelings**. Are you feeling any of those negative, non-productive feelings: anger, irritation, catastrophizing? If so, notice them and tell them to shut up. Sounds daft, but you really can talk to yourself in this way.

2. **Recognize your defensive response**. What do you actually do when you're being defensive? You might withdraw and exude an angry silence; you might try blaming or shaming others; you might try flooding others

with information to prove a point or to prove you're right. You might even experience a sudden drop in IQ. When we're feeling under threat, our higher cognitive functions, our IQ, can seriously plummet. Think about when someone called you out on something that had you caught red-handed. Those feelings of panic and fear are your brain's way of telling you that you're at risk. It's a flight or fight thing. It's a left-over primitive response whereby in flight or fight mode our brains shut down our higher cognitive functions so that we can quickly respond – without thinking – either run or fight. This is triggered by the release of cortisol, the stress hormone. Which, by the way, stays in our system for hours. Fast forward to the 21st century and of course the thing we need most when under pressure is the ability to think. So, the trick then is again to recognize the defensive response and to shut yourself up. Let yourself engage in an open way. This is completely self-trainable. And it really doesn't take long: spot the reaction, change it, and the more you do it, the quicker and more skilled you become. Which means that cortisol is not released, and you are able to respond in a level, measured way.

3. **Look for the truth in what's being said**. Don't get hung up on the bits of the challenge that you don't agree with. Actively look for what is correct. In case you haven't spotted it yet, all of this applies in exactly the same way at home as it does at work. When my wife challenges me, I've learned that if I'm having difficulty accepting the truth in what's being said (because my brain is really

busy, getting very indignant) I simply say 'I need to think about that. Give me a few minutes.' I then take those minutes and the space that quiet contemplation gives me to see the validity of the challenge. I then return to her and respond non-defensively. Honestly, it just makes you a better human being.

By the way, saying 'I need to think about that' and then not actually thinking about it, and not actually going back to that person with the results of your thinking, is a really good way to turn the heat up even more.

4. **Respond generously**. This doesn't mean saying things that you don't believe just to smooth things over. This means genuinely recognizing the value of the challenge and stating the positive value of that challenge to the person who challenged you. Neuropsychology is at play here too: being generous makes us feel good about ourselves and when we feel good, our levels of oxytocin are elevated. Oxytocin is a feel-good hormone that elevates our ability to communicate, collaborate and trust. However, oxytocin is metabolized much faster than cortisol – meaning that the negative effects we create last much longer than the positive effects. In our brains, negative experiences stick like Velcro, whereas positive ones tend to be more like Teflon. What that tells me is that I need fewer negative experiences in my life and lots more positive ones. That's not home-spun daft philosophy – I know that there will always be negative experiences in my life that I can't control. But I'm aware that being defensive means I'm responsible for creating

some of my own negative experiences. Why would I do that? And responding generously creates my own positive experiences. Why wouldn't I want to do that… a lot?

5. **Reflect on the response you got.** The final piece of the model is the part that shows that by going through this open cycle, it becomes self-fulfilling: the more we do it, the more these positive habits are formed and the easier it gets to respond openly rather than defensively. I'm working on this for myself. My first reaction to challenge used to be probably about 95% defensive responses. I reckon my first reaction being defensive is now at about 10% of the time. My goal is to get to zero because I've successfully re-wired my brain to instinctively respond differently.

Let's look at the self-coaching model with a real, personal example:

Someone has (dared to) critique my work…		
	Defensive response	**Open response**
1. ACKNOWLEDGE YOUR DEFENSIVE FEELINGS	Irritation/frustration/self-doubt	This might get a better result
2. RECOGNIZE YOUR DEFENSIVE RESPONSE	Dig your heels in to defend your work. Behave irritably. Question the quality of your other work	Stay level and non-judgemental
3. LOOK FOR THE TRUTH IN WHAT'S BEING SAID	You're wrong. My idea is better	They have some good points/good ideas
4. RESPOND GENEROUSLY	Withdrawal. Have a tantrum	Thank them (genuinely) for their feedback and make the required changes
5. REFLECT ON THE RESPONSE YOU GOT	Stalemate	It feels great to work in partnership with people who make our joint outputs better

Caring candour focus area 2: Candour with others

This might be the most important personal contribution you can make to changing culture rapidly. Let's say you've compellingly articulated why the culture needs to change and have described brilliantly the behavioural standards needed from everyone in order that they embody and embed the required culture. I've found that individuals often fall into three categories in response to this challenge to develop their behaviour:

- Got it. I know what's needed and will take a good hard look at myself to ensure I'm an exemplar of the target culture.

- Don't got it. I understand what's being asked of me, but I don't know if I either have the willingness or ability to change (e.g. 'I've been doing this for 30 years and retirement is approaching' or 'jeez, how the heck do I change a lifetime's worth of habits and learned behaviours?').

- Hope *they've* got it. I know exactly what others need to do. Luckily, I'm great and don't have to change a thing.

Unfortunately, the population size difference between (i) and (iii) is massive. Very few people seem to fit into the 'got it' category and large swathes of people fit into the 'hope *they've* got it' one.

The best tool we can apply to the 'don't got it' and the 'hope *they've* got it' folks is candour. Candidly providing feedback to those people about where the performance is strong and where it falls short and the impact that's having on teammates and the organization.

Let's recognize, though, that a number of people in the 'don't got it' category are suffering from imposter syndrome. They perceive themselves as being less good than they actually are. Feedback works with them too – because feedback should be given to reinforce good performance as well as to correct under-performance. More about that shortly.

But let's also recognize that some people are victim to the Dunning Kruger effect – in which they believe they're better than they actually are. Casting your mind around for an example? Look no further than the first politician that comes to mind.

The Dunning Kruger Effect and Imposter Syndrome

So, I'm going to focus on providing caring candour in the form of giving feedback – both to reinforce good performance and to correct poor performance. I know that, to use the British vernacular, we tend to think that a synonym for 'feedback' is 'bollocking'.[1] As in:

'Can I give you some feedback?'

'Oh shit, I'm going to get a bollocking.'

But there's also a famous phrase that describes the value of feedback far better, but often carries less weight than the getting sent to the Headteacher's office version. That phrase is:

'Feedback is the breakfast of champions.'

I love that. It turns the idea of feedback on its head. Feedback as a source of nourishment. Think again of Usain Bolt. He was the best sprinter on the planet that has ever lived. And yet he had a coach who gave him feedback. Why? Because feedback is the breakfast of champions. Because feedback helps us to improve.

However, many people brace themselves in the face of feedback. You can almost see them physically go rigid. The section about dropping your defences should help with that. However, many people also shrink from the idea of giving 'negative' feedback. They have some confused, messed-up version of what feedback is. They see it as unfriendly or unkind and might hurt someone's feelings. I see giving feedback as extremely friendly: to sit there thinking horrible thoughts about this person who has just let me down and *not* giving them feedback is decidedly unfriendly.

---

[1] Bollocks is the Swiss army knife of British expressions – you can use it in all sorts of ways, e.g. what you said is bollocks (nonsense); I've bollocksed it up (made a mistake); that move was bollocks (terrible). To get a bollocking is to be harshly scolded. Fabulous word – but don't use it with your grandparents.

I know you've likely been on Leadership Skills Training 101 where they talked about giving feedback. They perhaps taught you the daft version of giving feedback – the shit sandwich: say something nice, then say something horrible, then say something nice. Which is useless because the person on the receiving end either focusses only on the good stuff or only on the bad stuff.

I was talking to a good friend the other day who's a screenwriter for television. She was talking about being a Show Runner, which means the person who heads up the writers' room on a TV show or film. She described a world in which unwaveringly candid feedback isn't just helpful, but essential. They don't have the time to work around egos or under-performers. If they don't like an idea that one of the writers presents, they say so. If they like an idea, they dive in to build on it. It's instant, in-the-moment feedback. She went on to say that if someone gets defensive and leads with their ego, they're quickly removed from the writers' room. However, if the Show Runner is the person with the ego problem, it's a big issue. Because the writers end up going along with what they know is a sub-standard idea. But the Show Runners with big egos very quickly develop a reputation and, even if they wrote the original script, they're not appointed as Show Runners (which would be disappointing for them because working as a Show Runner pays a lot more than just writing the script).

So, let's talk about giving feedback *and* coaching support with caring candour to help people to improve. And let's never again refer to 'positive feedback' and 'negative feedback.' The purpose of *all* feedback should be to drive performance improvements.

Whether you need to get someone's performance from poor to good or from great to world-class.

Feedback with caring candour

As you read through this bit, have that phrase 'feedback is the breakfast of champions' squarely at the front of your mind. Your feedback should serve to nourish and grow the person getting the feedback. Feedback should not come from a place of anger. This is called dumping and it's for you, not them. Feedback should not come from an ego place: I need to prove that I'm right and they're wrong; I'm more important than them and I'm taking this opportunity to rub their nose in it. This is called being an arrogant arse.

PAIN statement: a tool to help you give difficult feedback

I've helped many leaders to overcome their innate anxiety about giving difficult feedback. It's incredibly common. Sometimes people don't want to give difficult feedback because it might upset the recipient, sometimes they don't want to give difficult feedback because they don't want the conflict that might arise. I get it. But, how much worse is it to leave an under-performer not doing their job properly and getting in the way of others doing their job?

The PAIN statement below is a tool to help you open a difficult conversation by giving clear, unambiguous feedback. Note that the acronym is pretty direct – talking to someone about the PAIN they're causing. But that's the point! Unless we're being direct, the feedback is unlikely to be effective and the recipient is unlikely to change. Even more importantly, candour builds trust. When you speak the truth in a caringly candid way, people learn that you say what you're thinking (in a respectful way). They know that when you give 'positive' feedback, you really mean it. They trust that if someone is letting the team down, you'll act. They trust that you won't ever let your ego or fear get in the way of doing the right thing. Plus, people know when you're pulling your punches – they've seen you pull your punches with other people, so they'll wonder if you're doing it with them.

P	Problem statement	A direct *opening statement* that frames the conversation
A	Action	The specific *action/behaviour* you've observed and want to discuss
I	Impact	What *impact* the actions/ behaviour had or is having on performance (either their own, yours, the team or the organization)
N	Next steps	State *where you'd like to get to next*: either by the end of the conversation OR as an end state

Here's an example:

P	Problem statement	I'd like us to talk about your completion against deadlines
A	Action	You committed to doing x, y and z over the last four weeks and you've failed to meet any of the deadlines you agreed to
I	Impact	In being late you are preventing others from completing their tasks
N	Next steps	I'd like to talk about why you're missing deadlines and agree a way forward so that this doesn't happen again

Here's another example:

P	Problem statement	I'd like to talk to you about your use of emails
A	Action	I've noticed you copy me in frequently on things I don't feel I need to be involved in
I	Impact	This is adding to my workload and reduces my capacity to support you in more constructive ways
N	Next steps	Let's work out together when its necessary for me to be copied in so that we can reduce the frequency and ensure I'm available when you do need my support

How to use the PAIN statement:

1. **Use it only to open the conversation.** It's not intended to be the entirety of the conversation. The N (next steps) is your entrée into an open conversation about the causes of the problem, mitigating factors and how to address the problem going forward.

2. **Script it in advance.** This will help you understand exactly what you want to say.

3. **It should take no more than 30 seconds to deliver.**

4. **Rehearse the script.** The more you rehearse a) the more it will come out in spoken English and won't sound like you've scripted it in advance; and b) the more comfortable you'll feel opening the difficult conversation.

5. **Seek first to understand.** Once you've delivered your PAIN statement, ask an open question to start a dialogue. And one of those open questions might be

to help them to think through, and you to understand, what's driving the performance deficit. You might give someone feedback that their absenteeism levels are very high. You might ask if there's anything going on that's compelling them to be absent. They might tell you about a sick relative or a difficult relationship. Understanding what's going on for them helps you to be compassionate when you should be or more authoritative when you need to be.

Here's another thought. With a small adaptation, you can use the same framework to give positive, reinforcing feedback. It works in exactly the same way:

G	Great stuff	I'd like to talk to you about your great performance at yesterday's presentation to the Executive Team
A	Action	You did a fantastic job of explaining the risks in the programme and it was clear you'd prepared well
I	Impact	The Executive Team didn't hesitate to agree the recommendations you put forward
N	Next steps	Let's take exactly that approach with the plan we're taking to them next month

I always suggest to leaders that they should be having a one-to-one with each of their Direct Reports at least once a month. This is often met with exasperation and spluttering noises: 'I don't have time for that; do you know how many people I've got reporting to me?!' First, having very big spans of control is a bad idea and should be dealt with through some organization re-design; let's leave that to one side for now. Second, despite their remonstrations, I insist. Unless you're speaking to each of your people regularly, how on earth are they supposed to know whether they're doing a good job? Waiting until the end of year appraisal to tell them (or perhaps to give them a conflict-avoidant view that they're doing OK) will not drive behavioural change and performance.

Your monthly one-to-ones might take 30 seconds: 'I'm really happy with everything you're doing and how you're going about it. Do you have anything you want to raise with me? No? OK, great job, carry on.'

Or your monthly one-to-ones might take an hour: 'Come in, shut the door, we need to have a long talk...'

Having said that, some feedback is best delivered in the moment rather than waiting for the formal one-to-one. The first PAIN statement above is a good example of this. This should be custom and practice – that when performance needs to be challenged now, the feedback is given now. And when great performance needs to be reinforced before the memory fades, the feedback is given now. My team and I customarily give each other feedback (in fact, we ask for it) after all key client interactions. We want to know each other's views about how we might have got a better result, and we also want to hear a jury of our peers tell us where we did a great job.

Providing coaching support with caring candour

I believe that coaching is one of the most critical leadership skills today. In fact, I won't hire anyone who isn't skilled in this or at least shows great interest and potential to do this. The world has moved on from people expecting to be told what to do and has moved to far greater levels of empowerment. We're more physically distant from each other with the post-Covid advent of home working. The market environments we work in change more rapidly now than ever before and we need to help our people to respond. People have far greater ability to move to new jobs, start their own businesses and build portfolio careers. Which means that it has never been truer that people join a great organization and leave a bad manager. People expect, in return for their dedication, to have the support of their manager in nurturing them and their careers. Coaching is therefore critical.

Here's the alternative to coaching people to improve their performance (again, whether it's from poor to good or from great to world-class): cross your fingers and hope for the best. Hope is not a strategy.

Having said that, recent research has demonstrated that hope manifests itself in the part of the brain associated with strategizing. Why? Because hope is all about showing us the possibilities. Not acting on those possibilities is hopeless. Helping yourself by acting to improve someone's performance is a hope strategy that works. Helping people to try some new ways of being, and being willing to fail fast, learn and go again, is a great hope strategy.

There are books and courses galore on coaching skills, so I won't go into detail here. But there are some fundamental principles to coaching that you should be aware of:

- **Coaching is not the same thing as mentoring.** Coaching means being able to help someone work something through without knowing anything much about the situation or the solution. My great friend who has been a coach to members of the Great Britain Olympic and Paralympic athletics teams can't do what they can do. He's never performed at anywhere near Olympic standard. And yet he's able to help them to win medals.

My team and I often do this coaching exercise with groups: we ask them to think about a situation that they would value spending about 20 minutes thinking through. We then ask the whole group about 20 questions and simply ask them to write down their answers. We don't ask them to tell us any of their answers. We have no idea what the answers are. The first bunch of questions help them to explore where they are now with their situation and what their goal is. The latter bunch of questions are intended to move them towards the actions they might take to achieve that goal. The last question we ask is how likely they are to take the action they've just decided to take on a scale of 1 to 10. Without hearing a single thing about what their situations are, or what their answers were, we ask them to call out what asking those questions did for them. Usually, the list of things that the questions made them do includes think, generate options, prioritize, think about the impact on others, see things from a different perspective and decide on a course of action. Every single time we do this, the first word that the group shouts out is 'think'. And that's the point, if you want people to think, coach them by asking questions. If you don't need their brain to show up, just tell them what to do.

- **Don't solutionize.** The temptation to jump in with a solution will be almost unbearable. After all, if you're in a leadership position, much of your job is to find solutions. You're good at solving problems, you've been promoted and got pay raises because of your ability to find the way forward. But that's not what coaching is about. If you tell someone what to do, they don't own it. And if it goes wrong, they can quite reasonably blame you. Asking high-quality questions to help them probe their thoughts and emotions will enable them to work out the best course of action. That's not to say that you should always 'ask' and never 'tell'. If there's genuinely one single solution and you know what it is, telling them what you need them to do is probably the most expedient thing to do. If there's smoke billowing under the door, you're not going to ask them what they think the carbon monoxide content of the smoke is. You're just going to tell them follow you out.

- **One of the best ways to learn how to coach is to have a coach yourself.** If you work with a talented coach, you'll learn a huge amount about the skills and mindset required. You'll learn how they encourage you to think about things in a completely different way; you'll see how they help you to understand your part in why the topic you're discussing came about; you'll witness how they help you find a progressive path while embracing all of the emotions you're feeling; and you'll notice that they do this without any judgement at all of you.

- **Get a coaching qualification.** If your employer will sponsor this, so much the better. It's such an incredibly valuable skill for the organization and for you that it warrants investing your time and (perhaps your) money in.

Caring candour focus area 3: Candour with the organization as a whole

Let's just recognize first that our current world environment does not expect honesty. I argued earlier that trust is a natural result of candour. And evidence from many different sources show that outside of our friends and family, there's not much trust around.

The UK Office of National Statistics reported in 2022 that only 20% of the UK population trusts political parties. Data from the Pew Research Center in the USA in 2023 revealed that trust in the Federal Government was at near record lows. Less than two in ten Americans said they trust the Government in Washington to do what is right 'just about always' (1%) or 'most of the time' (15%). This is among the lowest trust measures in nearly seven decades of polling.[2]

Yeah, but that's just politicians! Right? Wrong. A survey by LumApps of organizations in the UK, France and USA shows that only 20% of employees have 'full trust' in their company leadership.[3]

---

[2] Pew Research Center. Public Trust in Government: 1958–2023.

[3] www.lumapps.com/insights/press-releases/lumApps-research-only-25-of-uk-workforce-trusts-company-leadership/   (accessed February 2024).

Maybe that's not the case in your organization. Maybe there are high levels of trust where you work. In which case, great, you've got a strong base to build from. Whether there are low or high levels of trust in your organization, these principles for caring candour will go a long way to turning the trust dial to where it needs to be to deliver rapid culture change. If there are pre-existing low levels of trust, your people won't trust that you're serious about this, they won't trust that you'll do it right, they won't trust that you'll listen to them and they definitely won't trust that you'll be willing to take a long, hard look at yourself and change your own behaviours.

Two tips for demonstrating candour with the organization

1. **Fix known issues to demonstrate that you can be trusted.** As I've already mentioned, if you're aware of issues that your people have raised either recently or continuously over a period of time, fix them. If your employee opinion survey has thrown up the same issues year after year, if you know that some processes aren't fit for purpose anymore, if you know that support function X is not supporting, if you know that there are issues with your building(s), fix the problems. If you don't, you'll face two challenges: people will not trust that you're serious about the culture programme (or in fact, any kind of transformation/change programme) and when you launch your culture change programme, you'll swear you can feel the air disturbance caused by all the eye-rolling that goes on. They'll just wait for it to go away because they have evidence that you don't

keep your promises. Candidly saying you will fix them, candidly apologizing for not fixing them sooner, and then actually fixing them, will put you on a firm footing for culture evolution.

If you're not aware of issues that your people have been living with, find out what they are! Simply ask them to tell you what's getting in the way of them performing optimally. Categorize them, prioritize them and then put a dedicated team of your best people to work on fixing them. I bet you 50 bucks right now that most of the issues will be either people related (poor performers getting in their way) or processes that don't add value and/or that slow them down.

2. **Empower.** Decisions should be made at the lowest, most appropriate level. In other words, the people who know most about something should be able to make decisions and take action. Escalating for decisions is a productivity issue, a quality issue and a customer service issue. It's a productivity issue because decisions are being escalated into a bottleneck; it's a quality issue because decisions are being made by people with less information than the people who escalated; it's a customer service issue because it's a productivity issue *plus* a quality issue – customers are on the receiving end of slower, poorer quality decisions.

    Of course, it's not a free for all. Not everyone can make a decision about anything. You need to provide clear parameters for where decision-making authority sits.

What's this got to do with building trust? Because:

- Empowerment tells your people that you truly do need them, trust them, are interested in their views and happy for them to implement their ideas.
- It encourages you to be candid with yourself about where you're reluctant to relinquish control and candid with the people that you don't trust to make those decisions.

It was 26th March 2020, and I received a call from an old client asking me to come and help with the UK Government's emergency response to Covid. He had been appointed to lead the NHS's Nightingale Hospital Programme. Nightingale hospitals would be large facilities to treat Covid patients. Each Nightingale hospital would have about 5,000 beds and would relieve the pressure on already overwhelmed NHS hospitals. The Nightingale hospitals didn't exist. They would be created out of large conference centres and, in one case, a disused DIY superstore. At 5am the next morning, I arrived at the NHS headquarters in South London. The usually bustling building was a ghost town. Except for a few people in suits and a bunch of soldiers in uniform. The sight was pretty scary.

The Nightingale team consisted of 18 people – about half civilian and about half military. We had around two months to create about 20,000 new beds. We achieved this goal and largely this was due to brilliant leadership from the CEO (Sir Simon Stevens), COO (Amanda Pritchard – now the CEO of NHS England) and Chief Finance Officer (CFO) (Julian Kelly). They allowed us to operate on a principle of 'mission control and empowered execution'. Mission control meant they defined the goal, the mission – but not how to achieve it; empowered execution meant they let us get on with finding the best ways to achieve the goals. During those two months we didn't have to write any papers, we didn't have to attend any committee meetings, we were trusted to get it right and get it done. This seemingly simple method of operating drove a huge and rapid shift in NHS culture. From slow and bureaucratic, to fleet of foot and streamlined. The Nightingale team had a brilliant leader, who inspired the team to think about the art of the possible and deliver quickly (people were dying) whatever the obstacles. And the team was amongst the most talented I've ever worked with. This was not my usual gig. It was scary. We worked very long days and nights and I often lay awake in bed terrified that I'd made a poor decision that would result in the deaths of many people. At the same time, my culture change brain was observing what was happening and how it was happening with such extraordinary skill and speed. The Nightingale team had two huddles a day. Eighteen people who stood together – socially distanced – in the morning and afternoon to describe a) issues; and b) what they needed from others. We had to do this twice a day because things were moving so fast. The huddles didn't indulge in 'I did this yesterday' and 'on my agenda today...'. There was no time for that. Eighteen people did this in less than 30 minutes each time. There was, quite simply, no time for anything other than total candour. Candour gets things done. Candour binds people together. Candour cultivates trust within teams and across teams. I have no doubt that the CEO, COO and CFO would have stepped in if they felt they couldn't trust us. They were consistently candid with us, and we were consistently candid with them.

It was an extraordinary moment in my life. And I look back at it and reflect what can be achieved if you create a culture of mission control and empowered execution.

Culture can be changed and evolved rapidly if you can unify your people behind a compelling mission and let them find the best ways to execute. This requires candour from everyone: from leaders who might need to course correct and celebrate excellence, and from everyone else who knows that candour serves to accelerate mission completion while at the same time building extraordinary team bonds.

Chapter 11

Scheduling your culture change activities

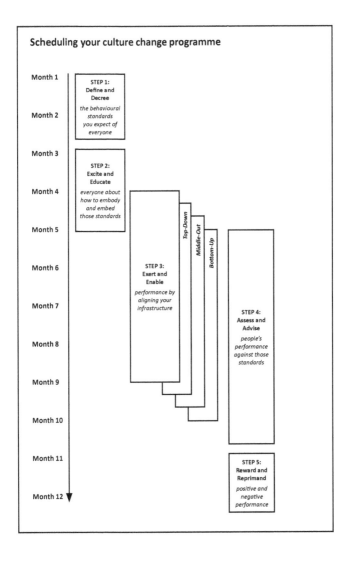

Scheduling your culture change programme

Hopefully, the first thing you'll probably notice about the schedule diagram is that it's fast. Obviously. I promised rapid culture change.

You must recognize that to do things in this timescale requires:

- **Proper commitment from the top**. That means that this is given the priority it needs amongst the other business priorities.

- **Resources**. Get these sorted before you start. The delivery resources, but just as important is the project management resources and really, really important is the administrative resources you'll need. There are lots of moving parts including sending invitations to middle-out sessions, collating RSVPs, booking rooms, setting up the 360 platform, sending invites to complete the 360 questionnaires, organizing one-to-one coaching, corralling the Executive Team to attend the team coaching sessions, etc., etc., etc. Underestimate the time needed for this administrative support at your peril. Meaning, if you don't find someone to do it, you'll end up doing it yourself.

Notice the staggered approach: you can start the top-down work in Empower and Enable before completing the Excite and Engage work for the whole organization, i.e. get cracking on getting the senior ducks in a row.

Don't start the middle-out work until the top-down work has started – so that you can be sure that when people look up, they'll recognize that everyone's on the same page. Same reason for starting the bottom-up work after you've started the middle-out work.

Start fixing infrastructure as soon as you have the information about what needs fixing. As mentioned earlier, you might already know some of this. In which case start on day one. As you collect more information about infrastructure enablers, get busy with those too.

You'll also notice that applying consequences for performance comes right at the end. This is the dignified way of doing things: make it clear to everyone what the performance expectations are, giving them time to learn and adapt and only then applying the positive and negative consequences.

Chapter 12

Summary of the key points/ stuff you can nick and claim as your own

That's OK – go ahead, take what you need. I mean, I haven't put it all into ready-made PowerPoint slides for you to copy and paste. You have to do some work yourself. But if I can help make your life easier, I'm in.

Ten points about rapidly changing your culture to dazzle and delight your CEO

1. The only reason to talk about culture is to determine whether it will help you to achieve your goals or get in the way. Culture is not a 'soft subject'.

2. Culture = behaviour PLUS infrastructure. Trying to change behaviours without tackling the processes, structures and systems that drives those behaviours is a waste of time.

3. It's about generating the multiplier effect of people not only doing their job brilliantly well but also enabling

everyone they work with to do their job brilliantly well too. It's all about performance.

4. The approach you need for effective and rapid culture change is:
   a. Top-down (get your senior ducks in a row)
   b. Middle-out (make sure your middle managers are engaged, committed and active)
   c. Bottom-up (drive performance improvements by getting the people who know most about where the obstacles are to identify them and remove them).

5. The silver bullet to deliver dramatic and rapid culture change is to apply positive and negative consequences for their performance.

6. The biggest obstacle to the introduction of a new culture is the old culture.

7. You must engage in positively-intended conflict through caring candour.

8. The people who need to change the most generally think they need to change the least, and people who think they need to change the least generally need to change the most.

9. Spend proper time and money on this or it won't work.

10. You have to deliver your culture change programme (as all change programmes) with pace in order to generate momentum.

Chapter 13

What do you do now?

Let's have a candid conversation. Before we talk, think about these things:

1. What's your gut instinct about how your culture is impeding performance?

2. What's good about your culture that you absolutely must keep?

3. If you had to boil down the essence of what needs to change about your culture, what are the top three things?

4. What resources do you have in-house to drive the culture change programme? How much bandwidth do they have to take on more responsibilities? If the answer is 'not much', what current responsibilities can you take from them to release some time – and either move those activities to someone else or shut them down (temporarily or permanently)?

5. What help do you need from me? A session with the Executive Team to help them focus on the importance of culture change? A talk about culture change at your next leadership conference? Support in scoping and

shaping a culture change plan? Resources to execute the culture change plan?

When you've spent a bit of time thinking about those questions, get in touch with me.

You can get in touch by going to www.innermost-consulting.com and going to the Contact Us section, or please email direct to info@innermost-consulting.com

About the author

Andrew Saffron is one of the world's leading culture change practitioners. His high challenge but engaging style has won him acclaim and awards. (They look nice on his office shelf next to his signed photo of Thierry Henry.)

He's worked with many global organizations, government departments and not-for-profit organizations to rapidly change their cultures. Some of these organizations have been in a flat spin, some have a performance level that's starting to plateau, and others were performing well and wanted to get even better.

He loves vinyl and football. He hates toffees and overly solicitous waiters.

Index

A quick word from Practical Inspiration Publishing...

We hope you found this book both practical and inspiring – that's what we aim for with every book we publish.

We publish titles on topics ranging from leadership, entrepreneurship, HR and marketing to self-development and wellbeing.

Find details of all our books at: www.practicalinspiration.com

 Did you know...

We can offer discounts on bulk sales of all our titles – ideal if you want to use them for training purposes, corporate giveaways or simply because you feel these ideas deserve to be shared with your network.

We can even produce bespoke versions of our books, for example with your organization's logo and/or a tailored foreword.

To discuss further, contact us on info@practicalinspiration.com.

 Got an idea for a business book?

We may be able to help. Find out more about publishing in partnership with us at: bit.ly/PIpublishing.

Follow us on social media...

 @PIPTalking

 @pip_talking

 @practicalinspiration

 @piptalking

 Practical Inspiration Publishing